Using the Visual Arts for Cross-curricular Teaching and Learning

D1555744

As schools are being encouraged to develop more flexible and creative approaches to education, *Using the Visual Arts for Cross-curricular Teaching and Learning* provides practical guidance and ideas on using the visual arts as a starting point for imaginative, effective learning across a wide range of curriculum subjects.

Underpinned by established and current educational thinking, it uses real-life examples to explore how this approach has been used successfully by individual class teachers and to inspire whole-school projects. Offering proven strategies supporting the principles of personalized learning, it will help you involve children in devising cross-curricular themes and setting their own lines of enquiry.

Supplemented throughout with case studies and ideas for great artworks to get projects started, as well as examples of children's own work, it explores:

- developing individual pupils' talent;
- using a single painting as a starting point for learning in a range of subjects;
- finding inspiration for your own cross-curricular projects using the visual arts;
- underpinning all activities with educational purpose;
- planning for and assessing progression in learning;
- discovering and using art resources in your region.

The tried and tested strategies in *Using the Visual Arts for Cross-curricular Teaching and Learning* will give all primary school teachers the confidence to explore the benefits of placing the visual arts at the centre of a creative, appealing curriculum.

Karen Hosack Janes is Visiting Lecturer in Education at the University of Northampton, and Associate Consultant for Chris Quigley Education Ltd, Newcastle, UK. Karen was previously Head of Schools at the National Gallery, London, UK, where she led a range of projects including the nationwide Take One Picture scheme. She was previously a teacher and Head of Art and Design in schools. She has written a number of books on art for children.

Using the Visual Arts for Cross-curricular Teaching and Learning

Imaginative ideas for
the primary school

Karen Hosack Janes

 Routledge
Taylor & Francis Group

LONDON AND NEW YORK

First published 2014
by Routledge
2 Park Square, Milton Park, Abingdon, Oxon OX14 4RN

and by Routledge
711 Third Avenue, New York, NY 10017

Routledge is an imprint of the Taylor & Francis Group, an informa business

British Library Cataloguing in Publication Data
A catalogue record for this book is available from the British Library

Library of Congress Cataloging in Publication Data
A catalog record for this book has been requested

ISBN: 978-0-415-50821-6 (hbk)
ISBN: 978-0-415-50825-4 (pbk)
ISBN: 978-0-203-12573-1 (ebk)

Typeset in Galliard and Gill Sans
by Florence Production Ltd, Stoodleigh, Devon, UK

Printed and bound in Great Britain by
TJ International Ltd, Padstow, Cornwall

Dedicated to my beloved husband Mark Janes.
Thank you for everything.

Contents

Acknowledgements

Kevin Brooks
Tony Cotton
Carol Ducker
Maggie Duroe
Brian Flynn
Mary Haig
Margot Henderson
Tish Keech
Mark and Lawrence Janes
Jennie McFadden
Del Rew
Sandra Sanders
Julie Shaughnessy
Jan Stoppani
Nick Sullivan
Jacqueline Wilson
Jan Young

Acknowledgement

Introduction

Children's visual development begins shortly after birth when they slowly start to focus their eyes on the shapes, patterns and contrasting tones of colour that form their new surroundings. From initially simply seeing, they then begin to recognize similarities and differences. As they mature, children start to communicate what they see in the world through the marks that they make, with crayons, pencils, chalks and paint – anything that comes to hand – simultaneously enjoying and investigating materials by building with bricks, modelling with sand, mud, dough and, of course, their food! This natural process of play-based learning expands an infant's experience. Through experience, their knowledge grows, influenced all the time by social interactions with family, friends and carers, and later also by the people that they meet in formal educational settings.

Young children's highly active sense of curiosity motivates them to ask many questions about what they observe in the world. Sometimes they verbalize these, with answers being requested from those around them. Other times, questions are non-verbal, resulting in self-generated explanations. Nurturing these skills, to think independently and collaboratively, and keeping eager children's early appetite for learning, is vitally important for their successful performance at school in all phases, and a principal challenge for teachers; one in which the visual arts can play a major role.

Children develop creative thinking skills through making artwork and by appreciating the artwork of others. Producing art helps children to explore their ideas in a way that is concrete, while looking at the paintings, drawings, sculptures, photographs and textiles, made by either contemporary artists or people from the past, helps to expand the imagination and acts as a central stimulus for developing questioning skills. For example, by asking, 'What is it?', 'Is it something familiar?', 'Do I like it?', children analyse what they see in terms of what they already know and decide on what needs more explanation. In a school setting, with skilful guidance from a teacher, an encounter with a work of art can lead to lively discussions and further enquiry, perhaps into something new and exciting, and perhaps into producing personal responses, maybe in the form of another visual artwork, or a piece of music or writing. In fact, the possibilities for this cycle of creativity are endless. One idea can inspire another, or many. These can be shared with more people, and in turn others can be inspired. It is an artistic process that connects people across time, place and cultures.

This book explores this artistic process in relation to pedagogy, highlighting the benefits of using the visual arts to help children make connections between subject areas and to develop key skills, such as literacy and numeracy skills, research, problem solving and evaluation skills, and presentation and personal development skills. Divided into three parts, the book first puts forward the case for the arts in general in education, summarizing recent relevant policies and reports. Then, in more detail, reasons for specifically integrating the visual arts across the curriculum are discussed, focusing on why they are such a powerful stimulus for teaching and learning. Part II illustrates, through examples of real-life practice, how the visual arts have been used very successfully as a central stimulus in projects that have given pupils opportunities to become fully immersed in activities that are personalized to their individual interests and needs, and at a level that has promoted growth in their learning. Many of these projects have also helped to foster a sense of community among pupils, year groups, teaching and non-teaching staff, and those beyond school, including parents and other schools (regionally, nationally and internationally). The final part aims to support teachers in designing their own cross-curricular projects through the visual arts. It discusses considerations from the initial planning stage to implementation, including selecting a work of art, resourcing, strategies for engaging interest among pupils, staff and parents, assessment, and ensuring progression.

Part I

Integrating the visual arts across the curriculum

The next two chapters, which make up Part I, put forward the case for the arts in education. They summarize some important policies and reports that have shaped arts education in schools and examine reasons for specifically integrating the visual arts across the primary curriculum, focusing on why they are such a powerful stimulus for teaching and learning.

Chapter 1

The case for the arts in education

The world is facing huge challenges, and they are growing daily in severity and in scale and complexity. It is no exaggeration to say that they are not going to go away; indeed, they will get worse unless we can start to find solutions, and soon. If we are going to survive, we desperately need the next generation to be smarter, more adaptable and better prepared than any that have gone before. Our only chance is to improve the way we teach our young – to equip young people with the skills and attitudes that might steer this world of ours to a far safer place than at present looks likely.

We are the people we've been waiting for.

(Rowland 2010)

This opening statement sets the scene for the 2010 documentary *We Are the People We've Been Waiting For*. Inspired by the McKinsey Report on Education (Barber and Mourshed 2007),[1] which compared 25 of the world's school systems, including 10 of the top performers, the film explores how many young people in the UK are not provided at school with the opportunities that they need to make the most success of their lives, and how ultimately this affects all our futures. The film supports the idea that pupils need to be given opportunities to develop creative thinking skills to become excellent problem-solvers, and that they need to enjoy and effectively work with other children and adults to hone their social skills and to become responsible citizens. It also highlights how young people need to learn about the world in which they live to actively evolve their own relationship with it. At a conference in 2006, run by the very well-respected non-profit organization TED,[2] Ken Robinson, Professor Emeritus at the University of Warwick, who appears in the film, proposed that education systems across the world favour models of learning that are not conducive to the conditions needed to prepare young people for the twenty-first century, going as far as saying that 'schools kill creativity' (the title of his talk) (Robinson 2006). He put forward the argument that children are educated out of creativity (which he defines as 'the process of having original ideas that have value') as they grow up because school systems prioritize those subjects that seem most relevant to the economy, where maths and languages are more highly valued than the humanities, and where the arts appear at the bottom of an education hierarchy. In his book *Out of Our Minds*, Robinson points out that 'Employers say they want people who can think creatively, who can innovate, who can communicate well, work in teams and are adaptable and self-confident'

(Robinson 2011: 69). These are the very skills that the arts can effectively develop, and they need to be given equal status to other subjects in our schools.

The importance of the arts in education has been a matter of protracted public and professional debate, particularly over the past 45 years. In 1967, the Plowden Report (Plowden *et al.* 1967), a wide-ranging review of primary education in England chaired by Lady Plowden and commissioned by the Conservative Education Minister Sir Edward Boyle in 1963, made this compelling statement:

> Art is both a form of communication and a means of expression of feelings which ought to permeate the whole curriculum and the whole life of the school. A society which neglects or despises it is dangerously sick. It affects, or should affect, all aspects of our life from the design of the commonplace articles of everyday life to the highest forms of individual expression.
>
> (Plowden *et al.* 1967: 248)

Recommendations from the report, although only partially implemented due to a change of government at the time of its publication, have been key in the development of the primary education system we have today. As well as articulating the crucial role of art in education, it promoted, among other ambitious ideas, parental participation in schools, and introduced the idea of educational priority areas to address issues of social disadvantage. It also set in motion the availability of nursery education for all 3- to 5-year-olds, prompted the end of the 11+ as a selection process for entering secondary education, and asked for regular reports evaluating the quality of education being taught in schools. These ideas are now widely viewed as desirable in a democracy that believes that every child has the right to a high-quality education. At the time of the report, when there were cuts in public expenditure due to recession, the lack of standardization across schools made many people nervous. Plowden strongly advocated a child-centred approach to learning, which essentially saw the teacher as an autonomous professional. However, with calls for schools to link their teaching more to the needs of the employment market, the 'great debate' around making mandatory a National Curriculum for all children between the ages of 5 and 16 was opened, outlined in 1976 by James Callaghan, Labour Prime Minister, in a speech at Ruskin College, Oxford.

The suggestion of state control over what children should learn in school was so controversial that it was not until 1988, under the Conservative administration lead by Margaret Thatcher, that the National Curriculum was established for England, Wales and Northern Ireland as part of the Education Reform Act.[3] Concerns over the place of the arts in a National Curriculum – what role they would play, if any – prompted the Calouste Gulbenkian Foundation to commission Ken Robinson, and others, to undertake a review of *The Arts in Schools* in the UK (Calouste Gulbenkian Foundation 1982). The final report aimed to challenge two misconceptions about the arts. The first being that 'the main role of education is to prepare young people for work', therefore making arts education 'unnecessary except for those looking for arts jobs', and second, that 'the arts had become associated with non-intellectual activities, and therefore seemed to lie outside the priorities of those who argued for a return to "traditional" academic values' (Calouste Gulbenkian Foundation 1982: xii). Widely acclaimed for presenting the case for the arts in terms of being essential to the general purpose of education, the report argued that the arts should be taught as part of a broad and balanced curriculum. It described ways in which the arts make a vital contribution to the personal development of children, as well as having long-term economic and social benefits for the country. *The Arts in Schools* discussed how the arts appeal to the full range of human intelligence (a subject focused on by Professor Howard Gardner, Harvard Graduate School of Education, in his theory of Multiple Intelligences, which I will come back to later), thus allowing for a more effective experience of education for a greater number of pupils. The report detailed how the arts provide a means of expression to organize thoughts and feelings about the world in which children live and how the arts promote an understanding of cultural change. It recommended that 'creative thought and action should be fostered in all areas of education' and how 'In the arts they are central' (Calouste Gulbenkian Foundation 1982: 11).

Fortunately, the arts were included in the 1988 National Curriculum, although the structure of it, and where the arts were placed, produced problems that are still evident today. Subjects were divided into 'core' and 'foundation', with the core subjects – English, Maths and Science – being used as key indicators of educational standards. The implication was that the foundation subjects – Art, Music, Physical Education, Technology, History and Geography (and a modern foreign language from age 11) – were of lower importance, and as such fewer hours were allocated to them by schools, although the amount of time spent on any subject was not stipulated in the statutory requirements. The legacy of this two-tiered model has meant that specialist expertise in foundation subjects has been given a lower priority than for core subjects. The arts have been particularly affected by this, attracting minimal Continuing Professional Development (CPD) training provision, and sometimes even being dropped from Initial Teacher Education (ITE) courses altogether.

Undermining the foundation subjects further, 10 years after the establishment of the National Curriculum, schools were granted permission from the then Labour government to suspend the requirements for the foundation subjects in order to make time to embed the new frameworks for the National Literacy Strategy (DfEE 1998) and National Numeracy Strategy (DfEE 1999), which were part of the Governments's drive to improve standards. In what seems like a strangely timed move, Ken Robinson was simultaneously invited to chair the National Advisory Committee on Creative and Cultural Education (NACCCE) by the Secretary of State for Education and Employment, David Blunkett, and the Secretary of State for Culture, Media and Sport, Chris Smith. The NACCCE, which included highly respected members from the education, business and arts and entertainment sectors, was asked 'to make recommendations to the Secretaries of State on the creative and cultural development of young people through formal and informal education: to take stock of current provision and to make proposals for principles, polices and practice' (NACCCE 1999: 2). The report, entitled *All Our Futures: Creativity, Culture and Education*,[4] basically highlighted the same key messages about the arts that were put forward in *The Arts in Schools*, contextualizing them within an examination of creative education, favouring 'a democratic conception of creativity: one which recognizes the potential for creative achievement in all fields of human activity; and the capacity for such achievements in the many not the few' (NACCCE 1999: 30). In addition, the report articulated unease with the general enduring debates around education itself:

Over a number of years, the balance of education, in our view, has been lost. There has been a tendency for the national debate on education to be expressed as a series of exclusive alternatives, even dichotomies: for example as a choice between the arts or the sciences; the core curriculum or the broad curriculum; between academic standards or creativity; freedom or authority in teaching methods. We argue that these dichotomies are unhelpful. Realising the potential of young people and raising standards of achievement and motivation includes all of these elements.

(NACCCE 1999: 9)

John Dewey, American philosopher and acknowledged pre-eminent educational theorist of the twentieth century, drew attention to this problem in educational philosophy over 60 years earlier. He recognized in his essay *Experience and Education* how 'Mankind likes to think in terms of extreme opposites' (Dewey 1938: 17) and described the extreme characteristics of traditional and progressive forms of education. The former he portrayed as a method that transmits bodies of information that have been worked out in the past to a new generation via textbooks, where teachers deliver the material and the attitudes of the pupils must be one of 'docility, receptivity and obedience' (Dewey 1938: 18). The latter he outlined as a set of principles that emphasize 'the freedom of the learner' (Dewey 1938: 22), which have been developed purely as a rejection of the traditional system. Dewey noted that simply reacting against old-fashioned ways of teaching did not address the fundamental problem that many pupils encountered in their schooling, namely disengagement.

Fundamental to Dewey's philosophy of education is 'the organic connection between education and personal experience' (Dewey 1938: 25). Although not suggesting that within a traditional classroom no experiences take place, he described them as, in the main, poor quality and 'mis-educative' (Dewey 1938: 25), meaning they have a negative impact on future learning – turning pupils off their education – echoing Ken Robinson's view that 'schools kill creativity'. Dewey talks about high-quality learning experiences resulting from teaching approaches that promote experimentation, sensitivity and inquisitiveness. This leads to pupils making connections with further experiences, therefore ensuring growth; a principle that Dewey calls the experiential continuum, more widely known today as experiential learning, a concept that I will return to in the next chapter. It can be said with certainty that teaching and learning through the visual arts, and the arts in general, encourages experimentation, sensitivity and inquisitiveness, and therefore these subjects embody the characteristics needed for high-quality educational experiences to take place.

What and how teachers teach will always be a political football as successive governments attempt to solve problems in society through educational reform.

However, the fundamental issue to be addressed is always the same: how best can we motivate learners in wanting to learn? If a significant level of interest is not present in an individual, then progress is unlikely, or at least diminished.

Two recent substantial reviews of the National Curriculum, the Rose Review (Rose 2009), commissioned by the Labour government, and the Cambridge Primary Review (CPR) (Alexander 2010), funded by the Esmee Fairbairn Foundation, have stressed the importance of the arts in a curriculum that supports deep engagement, with the impact being an improvement in overall educational performance. Both reviews warn that the National Curriculum should be truly broad and balanced and not be too overloaded in order to allow teachers the time and the flexibility to shape learning around the needs of the children at individual schools. 'The trend – usually motivated by the desire to strengthen particular aspects of learning – has been to add more and more content with too little regard for the practicalities and expertise needed to teach it effectively' (Rose 2009: 3).

In a government press release on 20 January 2011, the coalition expressed their intentions to tackle this overload with a review of the National Curriculum, effective in schools from 2014. In slimming down the content to reflect 'the body of essential knowledge all children should learn' but 'not absorb the overwhelming majority of teaching time in schools', concerns around the role of the arts in education have re-emerged once again, as have general anxieties over how much freedom teachers are afforded in designing their learning objectives around the needs of their pupils and making the curriculum as engaging as possible for everyone. During the drafting and consultation phase, Michael Gove, the Secretary of State for Education, wrote to Tim Oats (on 11 June 2012), the chair of the expert panel presiding over the review, and Director of Research and Assessment at Cambridge Assessment, stating that he wanted the new curriculum to encourage:

> a love of education for its own sake, respect for the best that has been thought and written, appreciation of human creativity and a determination to democratise knowledge by ensuring that as many children as possible lay claim to a rich intellectual inheritance.[5]

Few would argue with these goals; however, the question over what constitutes 'essential knowledge' is subjective and dependent on one's own personal beliefs and interests. Do we all believe the same knowledge is essential? Is some knowledge more essential than other knowledge? Who should choose what knowledge is essential for all the nation's children to learn about? How often should this be reviewed? What might influence what is selected? Does viewing education in this way lose sight of the fundamental issue of engaging children in their learning and helping them to make progress?

Those with an interest in the arts[6] fear, as I do, that compelling evidence from previous reports, surveys and reviews,[7] and even the findings of an independent review on cultural education in England commissioned by the coalition (known as the Henley Review) (Department for Culture, Media and Sport & Department for Education 2012) have been overlooked in favour of a more traditionalist agenda. A National Curriculum that focuses too strongly on information that has been worked out in the past at the expense of valuing the educational purpose of developing creative skills, and how these skills are transferable to the workplace, and how the arts can help pupils fully engage in their education, risks many children becoming switched off from their learning.

Art and Design is included in the reviewed National Curriculum, although the image of a broad and balanced curriculum, advocated by the Plowden and NACCCE reports and the Rose Review and CPR, has not been completely upheld, as Dance and Drama are not subjects in their own right. This omission will inevitably lead to a lack of parity of opportunity for children across the country in these subject areas and less funding being made available for them for CPD and ITE training when competing with other mandatory subjects.

The question for Art and Design now is whether enough detail is provided in a slimmed down National Curriculum for non-specialists to realize the limitless possible benefits the visual arts can have for developing social and personal skills and for making learning more meaningful and engaging across the curriculum. The next chapters aim to address a lack of specialist knowledge by offering teachers tried and tested strategies for introducing the visual arts in the classroom without the need for previous knowledge of art-making or Art History. The aim is to give teachers the confidence to learn alongside their pupils and to appreciate the advantages of placing the visual arts at the centre of a creative curriculum that draws together shared keys skills and concepts from other disciplines.

Notes

1   The McKinsey Report on Education, *How the World's Best-performing Schools Come Out on Top* (Barber and Mourshed 2007), compared 25 of the world's school systems, with the aim of understanding how different countries structure their education systems and which achieve pupil outcomes most capable of meeting the fast-growing global demand for high-level skills and knowledge. *How the World's Most Improved School Systems Keep Getting Better* (Mourshed *et al.* 2010) is a follow-up report. Both are available online at: http://mckinseyonsociety. com/topics/education/. McKinsey & Company is a global management-consulting firm.

2   TED is a non-profit organization, started in 1984, which aims to bring together people from the worlds of Technology, Entertainment and Design through a website and two annual conferences held in Long Beach/Palm Springs, USA, and Edinburgh, Scotland.

3   The Education Reform Act 1988 is available at www.legislation.gov.uk/ukpga/1988/40/ pdfs/ukpga_19880040_en.pdf (accessed 12 September 2013).

4   Also known as the Robinson Report.

5   The letter is available at: http://media.education.gov.uk/assets/files/pdf/l/secretary% 20of%20state%20letter%20to%20tim%20oates%20regarding%20the%20national%20curriculum %20review%2011%20june%202012.pdf (accessed 12 September 2013).

6   The Cultural Learning Alliance (CLA) is one of the strongest advocacy voices, with members from the cultural sector and arts education sector, and partners including Arts Council England and the Calouste Gulbenkian, Clore Duffield and Paul Hamlyn Foundations – all major grant-giving organizations for the arts.

7   In particular, those already mentioned in the book, namely the Plowden Report (Plowden *et al.* 1967), *The Arts in Schools* (Calouste Gulbenkian Foundation 1982), *All Our Futures: Creativity, Culture and Education* (NACCCE 1999), *How the World's Best-performing Schools Come out on Top* (Barber and Mourshed 2007), the Rose Review (Rose 2009) and the Cambridge Primary Review (Alexander 2010).

Chapter 2

Why the visual arts are such a powerful stimulus for teaching and learning

To be honest, when I was at school, I was not really interested in the work of artists. The faded and battered posters that were an attempt to adorn my school corridors included the usual suspects from Art History. Constable's *Hay Wain* (1821) did not get my pulse racing, da Vinci's *Mona Lisa* (*c.*1503–6) did not speak to me, and to this day I do not understand why van Gogh's *Sunflowers* (1888) is so popular – a vase of dead flowers, how depressing.

Luckily, I was good at drawing (I still have the intricate studies that I made of tree roots, and I am amazed at how much patience I had then). I also loved ceramics and making batik hangings, and when I was taking my A levels in the sixth form, I was granted permission to go to life drawing classes at the local adult education centre. It was there that I found out about the beautiful paintings of Gustav Klimt and Pierre Bonnard, and Auguste Rodin's exquisite sculptures of the human figure. I was hooked for life.

Later, when I was at art school, I went to the National Gallery in London and was blown away by the magnificent Renaissance altarpieces and the fantastic storytelling in the epic mythological images. I even came across Constable's *Hay Wain* (1821) again (the real one this time) and was taken aback by its large size. I noticed that it was a lush green colour, not dirty brown, and that the clouds looked so real that they almost moved across the canvas. I was pleasantly intrigued at how much I liked it and how relaxing it was to gaze at. I pondered in front of it for a while, thinking about what the people in the painting might be saying to each other, and wondered why these sources of rich inspiration had only just been presented to me in this way. Something dawned on me at that moment that seems so obvious to me now: seeing the original of a work of art is crucially important to fully appreciating it. First, the scale of an original work of art is something that is difficult to convey in a poster, in a book or on the Internet. Similes can be used to convey that a sculpture is bigger than three double-decker buses, or a miniature portrait is the size of a postage stamp, but until you see the real thing, the enormity or delicacy of a work of art is hard to imagine. Also, being able to look directly at the brushstrokes or carving marks made by an artist almost wipes away time – he or she actually made *those* marks – they took pleasure in making them, or alternatively agonized over them. It can be awe-inspiring to be in the presence of an artwork superstar. And finally, rarely are the colours and the textures of the materials transferred authentically to a reproduction; you have to see these in the flesh. Although, it has to be said, with advances in digital imaging technology, colour matching can now be superb and sometimes the viewer is able to see details in a printed or virtual reproduction that the naked eye can not in the original (for example, in a 'zoomable' image on the Internet).

Years later, after teaching in schools, making sure that my pupils were familiar with the wonders of the world of art, I had the chance to work in the Education Department at the National Gallery. I hugely enjoyed taking groups of school pupils on themed tours, sitting or standing them in front of 'the real thing', asking them about what they saw in the paintings, showing them how to 'read' visual symbols to unravel meaning, and helping them to make connections between different works of art. It was there that I experienced how much most children and young people love to 'interact' with art, expressing their ideas with an ease that sometimes surprised their teachers. It was apparent that art really can switch pupils on.

So, why do pupils feel so comfortable with looking and talking about images and artefacts? It is because they have been honing their visual skills since they first opened their eyes. By noticing similarities and differences, they develop the ability only after a few days of being born to differentiate between the face of their mother and other family members. As parents, we stimulate this development in babies by placing a mobile over a baby's cot, decorating bedrooms with bright colours and shapes, and buying toys and books with different textures and exciting noises. Through their senses, children begin to build their knowledge of the world, recognizing sights, exploring materials and listening to sounds.

How knowledge and understanding are acquired through interactions with the environment is the subject of constructivism, a theory of knowledge with roots in philosophy and psychology. Jean Piaget (1952), the hugely influential Swiss epistemologist, observed that knowledge is not something we are born with or that comes to children in a fully realized form; rather, it is something that must be seen in action over a long period of time and be constructed by the individual. Internal cognitive structures, which he called *schema*, evolve from birth to adulthood through means of adaptation to the external environment. Schema are sets of reflexive, at first, and later mental processes that form an increasingly complex network of knowledge and understanding. The child moves between the process of *assimilation*, which leads to classifying new stimuli into existing schema, and *accommodation*, which leads to creating new schema or modifying existing schema. Both of these change the child's individual perception of his or her environment; a journey that continues as he or she matures at varying speeds depending on the person. Piaget's theory explains how children learn and why they are motivated to learn more. When either new schema are created or old ones modified, *equilibrium* is achieved, and progression made. *Disequilibrium* occurs when there is imbalance between assimilation and accommodation (known as *cognitive conflict*), and this results in the child wanting to find out more and to question his or her own thinking, making children active participants in their own learning.

This Piagetian understanding of how knowledge is constructed is key to the philosophy of the internationally acclaimed Reggio approach. This has evolved from the preschools of a small city in the Emilia Romagna region of northern Italy, where, after the devastation of the Second World War, the citizens sought to empower their children in a style of learning that would enable the community to positively move forward. The approach, which has a growing following across the world, places great emphasis on children, teachers and their parents learning from first-hand experiences, and generating their own questions to be used as starting points for further investigation. Children are able to learn about the world in a way that is shaped around their own interests and prior knowledge, therefore naturally motivating them in wanting to find out more; a truly experiential way of learning, as John Dewey would describe it (Dewey's theories also greatly influenced the development of the approach, as did the work of Jerome Bruner, Lev Vygotsky and Howard Gardner, all of whom I look at later). With no predetermined curriculum, Reggio children (as they are known) are involved in steering short- and long-term projects that are nurtured by a practising artist who works alongside other teachers. Children and adults are encouraged to research, investigate and create in the *artelier* (a studio workshop area) and express themselves using 'a hundred languages', as explained in a poem by Loris Malaguzzi, the inspiration behind the educational experience (translated by Lella Gandini):

No way. The Hundred is There

The child
is made of one hundred.
The child has a hundred languages
a hundred hands
a hundred thoughts
a hundred ways of thinking
of playing, of speaking.
A hundred always a hundred ways of listening
Of marvelling, of loving
a hundred joys
for singing and understanding
a hundred worlds
to discover
a hundred worlds
to invent
a hundred worlds
to dream.
The child has
a hundred languages
(and a hundred hundred hundred more)
but they steal ninety-nine.
The school and the culture
Separate the head from the body.
They tell the child:
to think without hands
to do without head
to listen and not to speak
to understand without joy
to love and to marvel
only at Easter and at Christmas.
They tell the child:
to discover the world already there

and of the hundred
they steal ninety-nine.
They tell the child:
that work and play
reality and fantasy
science and imagination
sky and earth
reason and dream
are things
that do not belong together.
And thus they tell the child
That the hundred is not there.
The child says:
No way. The hundred is there.

(Thornton and Brunton 2009: 17)

One way that children reveal their perceptions and questions about their environment is in their drawings. Instinctively, as soon as they can hold a pencil, a piece of chalk, a crayon or paintbrush, children start to experiment with making marks. This is the beginning of visual self-expression and from here they progress through stages that match their cognitive development. Georges-Henri Luquet (1913) first introduced this concept in *Les Dessins d'un Enfant*, which was developed further by Viktor Lowenfeld (1947) and Herbert Read (1958), among others. In general, from around 14 months old, a child will enjoy scribbling. From these scribbles, shapes and images slowly emerge, such as circles, zigzags and crosses. As the lines become more controlled, the shapes might be named by the child as a person or object (for example, 'mummy' or 'a tree'; see Figure 2.1). This is the start of a stage when attempts are being made to draw realistically. As the child repeats the drawings, together with being influenced by the drawings of other people (their peers, family members, preschool and school teachers, and illustrations in books), a system of visual symbols emerges. These are more conceptual than based purely on observation, and reveal much about how children feel about their world, as well as showing what they know. Significant people in their lives may be drawn larger than others, parts of the body that are related to experiencing the world, such as the head, eyes, hands and fingers, are larger, and sometimes objects are shown from the inside as well as the outside. When children mature and become more self-aware of their technical abilities, they strive to depict people and objects more as they see them in real life, using conventions such as perspective to indicate space and depth in a picture. But sadly, the unrestrained naivety and spontaneity in children's artwork can be lost at this stage, and in many cases a decline in interest in art can take place when they start to believe that they are 'no good at drawing'. How many times have I heard those words from older children, young people and adults? However, it is perfectly possible to teach drawing skills and, if practised and matched with the willingness to observe what is actually seen, and not what the person who is drawing thinks that he or she sees, then drawing abilities can be significantly improved (see Part III for some simple activities that aim to improve confidence in drawing).

Figure 2.1 'Mummy' by Lawrence, age 4.

The following findings were reported by Ofsted in *Making a Mark: Art, Craft and Design 2008–11*:

> Almost all children in the EYFS [Early Years Foundation Stage] who spoke with inspectors said they liked drawing. This was reflected in the way many gravitated to drawing activities when selecting tasks for themselves.
>
> (Ofsted 2012a: 60)

> However, inspection findings highlighted that the notion that 'everyone can draw' is not being kept alive beyond the early stages of schooling. Discussions with pupils across the primary school age range revealed that many pupils' confidence in drawing diminished incrementally as they got older. Pupils who had lost interest in drawing usually perceived that they were not good at it, especially in recording appearances accurately.
>
> (Ofsted 2012a: 61)

> Teachers' subject expertise in drawing varied widely. In primary schools, teachers' lack of confidence in their own drawing abilities meant they were reluctant to demonstrate drawing techniques to pupils and to assess pupils' progress.
>
> (Ofsted 2012a: 62)

Drawing is the starting point for most works of art and, in some cases, the final piece as well. Therefore, it is well worth teachers practising their own skills in drawing to enable them to support their students in this area. If respected and encouraged, the gift that children have to express themselves in their drawings can be extended into other media (painting, printmaking, modelling, photography, textiles) and hopefully lead to a lifelong interest in the visual arts as well.

Encouraging self-expression and developing a lasting aesthetic awareness can be simultaneously improved through making strong connections between pupils making their own artwork and learning about the artwork of others. This should include both highly accomplished pieces by artists from the past and by contemporary artists, perhaps working alongside children in the school. In any field of learning, we need to look at those who excel in their area to give us insight into what is possible, and what constitutes high quality. Children need to learn about the creative processes of producing such artwork and how it relates to their own practice.

Self-expression and visual communication are, in essence, what art is all about. Just as young children explore art materials and grapple with learning about the world and their relationship with it through visual representations, so do older artists who create art for pleasure or as a career. Through their media of choice, artists deal with the universal themes that affect human beings, such as birth, death, love and beauty. Thousands of works of art from all over the world across different centuries can illustrate this. Pablo Picasso depicts his response to the bombing of a small Basque town during the Spanish Civil War in his masterpiece *Guernica* (1937). Edvard Munch's *The Scream* (1895) shows a lone figure, overcome by emotion, standing on a bridge in a violent red landscape. Artists explore ideals of beauty by studying and depicting nature, as in Leonardo da Vinci's exquisite botanical drawings and Claude Monet's paintings of his gardens at Giverny in France. The force of nature and the sublime captivates artists too, seen in the woodblock print of *The Great Wave of Kanagawa* (1831) by the Japanese artist Hokusai, and the work of Casper David Friedrich in the early nineteenth century. And religious and mythological works of art, by artists including Botticelli and Tintoretto from the time of the Renaissance, try to deal with difficult questions about why and how we are here, telling stories to explain theories and beliefs. Indeed, if we are looking for an answer to the age-old question, 'What is art?', it is somewhere to be found within our innate human need to express our feelings to others about how we fit into a wider scheme.

Because humans like to communicate important ideas through their art, we can examine it to try to learn about people from our own time and from the past. This might be about the artists themselves or the people and things that they have depicted. As Steve Seidel, Director of the Arts in Education Program at Harvard Graduate School of Education, explains, 'If we want to understand the values, morals, philosophies, aesthetics, and qualities of life in an historical period or geographic region (including our own), we study the arts of that time and place' (in Deasy 2005: vi). As a cornerstone of a civilized society, the arts are a good source of information about the politics of the day, containing clues about power struggles, wealth and attitudes to modernity. Portraits of kings and queens tend to clearly display symbols of affluence and authority, as do portraits of emperors and dictators. Changing attitudes to royalty post-French Revolution forced subsequent portraits of many royal families in Western Europe to be more conciliatory, echoing in visual form a new era. Advances in technology over the centuries can be seen in works of art too. For example, Joseph Mallord William Turner's *Rain, Steam and Speed – The Great Western Railway* (1844) celebrates the advent of the steam train. L.S. Lowry's industrial landscapes give an impression of what life was like for many people living in urban centres between the late 1920s and the 1970s, and *The Ambassadors* (1533) by Hans Holbein the Younger positively flaunts what was cutting edge at the time of Henry Tudor.

Some artworks can even mentally transport the viewer to the time and place they were made. A wonderfully clever example of this is Joseph Wright of Derby's life-size masterpiece *An Experiment on a Bird in the Air Pump* (1768). In it, he provides a place at the table for the viewer to pull up a chair and participate in watching an eighteenth-century scientist demonstrating how a vacuum is formed, at the expense of a bird he is starving of oxygen. The artist concentrates on the reactions of each individual in the small audience. As a viewer of the artwork, and a member of the same audience, we have to 'read' the facial expressions and decide what people are thinking. By involving us so intimately, the artist is asking what we think about the experiment too. The message being shared by Joseph Wright of Derby is that some people at the time were less enthusiastic about scientific advances than others, many of whom would have been cautiously debating questions of religious faith and ethical issues.

The visual arts are a mine of information about people and communities – what they are proud of, what they love and fear and aspire to. Children's natural inclination to use the arts as a language (Malaguzzi 1998) makes looking at a diverse range of artworks very appealing for them. By doing so, teachers can significantly contribute to the way children learn about the world, extending and challenging their ideas, knowledge and understanding, and sparking their vivid and limitless imaginations.

For children, there is no huge leap between looking at a Renaissance masterpiece and an illustration in a picture book. They expect to unpack what they see, seeking to find a narrative. Often independently, they guess who someone in a picture might be from what they are wearing or holding. They take delight in predicting what might happen next and they make assumptions about whether the artwork shows the 'olden days' or if it is from their own time. This freedom for interpretation is very engaging to children. However, as adults, we may feel that there is a correct way to look at art, and this can make us uncomfortable – we might resist the temptation to express what we think about a work of art so not to risk being embarrassed that we might be 'wrong'. But the real truth is there is never just one way of looking at a work of art.

We all bring to a work of art our own experiences and beliefs and, as with reading a book or any other activity that stimulates our imagination, our interpretations are unique to us. Even if the story that is being told in an artwork is clear (as in, for example, a nativity scene), for others (perhaps non-Christians), the main attraction of the piece might be the stunning use of gold leaf in the angels' halos or the beautiful way each animal has been painted or sculpted. An image with horses in a landscape will have a different impact on an equestrian expert than it would on a farmer, each being interested in what they know best about. A girl who loves ballet would be fascinated by the bronze cast of Edgar Degas's *Little Dancer Aged Fourteen* (1880–1; cast *c*.1922) for different reasons to a fashion designer, who might be more captivated by the use of fabric. All their viewpoints would be personal perspectives and each would be valid.

The ways in which works of art enable people of all ages and abilities to have their own unique responses, while at the same time offering many opportunities to learn about the world and other cultures, makes the visual arts ideally suited for cross-curricular teaching and learning. This approach contributes meaningfully to pupils' spiritual, moral, social and cultural development. It can be especially effective in primary schools where cross-curricular projects are used to help pupils demonstrate and perfect their skills, knowledge and understanding that they have learnt in subject areas which have been taught discretely. At the same time as meeting Art and Design learning objectives, with pupils finding out about the artistic processes of exploring a theme and experimenting with techniques and making strong links between their own art-making and the work of others, a host of other skills and knowledge specific to other subject disciplines (but crucially transferable to others) can be acquired. For instance:

Literacy – Listening and responding critically to artworks as 'texts'; talking confidently about ideas and listening to others; presenting ideas in different forms (including using ICT); analysing meaning.

Numeracy – Understanding the properties of shapes (2D and 3D), including symmetry, rotation and repeated patterns.

Computing – Finding and selecting virtual images and information on the Internet and making judgements about accuracy; sharing work with different audiences beyond the school by being involved in online projects; using technology to produce digital images (including film and animation).

History and Geography (the Humanities) – Undertaking investigations and perusing lines of enquiry using the visual arts as an initial stimulus; analysing and interpreting different sources of information; debating opinions.

Science – Developing first-hand observational drawing skills to investigate and record accurately; investigating the properties of materials through experimentation; using visual representations to illustrate how science works; evaluating these in their historical contexts.

Music, Dance and Drama – Using the visual arts as a starting point for creating work in another art form.

In Part III, I discuss in more depth how transferable skills, including the basic skills of literacy and numeracy, and skills involved in researching, problem-solving, evaluation, presentation, thinking independently and displaying a positive attitude to learning, can be developed across the curriculum using the visual arts as a central stimulus.

Real or perceived restrictions with a National Curriculum have sometimes been seen as barriers to cross-curricular teaching and learning in primary schools, although findings from Ofsted, published in *Learning: Creative Approaches that Raise Standards,* surveying 44 schools across all phases that use creative approaches demonstrate that this does not have to be the case:

> Pupils who were supported by good teaching that encouraged questioning, debate, experimentation, presentation and critical reflection enjoyed the challenge and had a sense of personal achievement. The confidence they gained encouraged them to develop and present their own idea with greater imagination and fluency. Approaches developed successfully in traditionally 'creative' subjects, such as the arts and English, were often incorporated into other areas, such as science and mathematics . . . In schools with good teaching, there is not a conflict between the National Curriculum, national standards in core subjects and creative approaches to learning.
>
> (Ofsted 2010: 5)

A recommendation in Ofsted's *Making a Mark: Art, Craft and Design 2008–11* (Ofsted 2012a: 7) noted that links with related areas of the curriculum tended to be underdeveloped and that schools should build more on pupils' experiences and creative development in the Early Years Foundation Stage (EYFS) in primary and secondary schools, something I would wholeheartedly agree with.

In the EYFS, learning is underpinned by the themes *a unique child, positive relationships* and *enabling environments* (Department for Education 2012a). It promotes a holistic approach to learning for children aged 0–5, breaking down (or, more accurately, not building up) the artificial dividers the National Curriculum puts between subject areas in the subsequent phases. This helps children to learn more effectively, constructing links between prior knowledge and new experiences (as discussed in Chapter 1). Across seven interconnected areas of learning (Personal, social and emotional development, Communication and language, Physical development, Literacy, Maths, Understanding the world, Expressive arts and design), the structure of the EYFS framework enables 'children to explore and play with a wide range of media and materials' and it encourages the sharing of children's 'thoughts, ideas and feelings through a variety of activities in art, music, movement, dance, roleplay, and design and technology'. Teachers provide children 'with opportunities to develop a positive sense of themselves' and 'to have confidence in their own abilities', 'to make sense of their physical world and their community' and have 'respect for others'. Although not placing the arts at the centre of the framework, like the Reggio approach, the EYFS acknowledges that the visual arts are fundamental in being able to achieve these aims.

The relatively new area of neuroscience can additionally aid our understanding of why it is so important to give children opportunities to make numerous links between things that they encounter on a regular basis, and hence why teaching in a cross-curricular way through stimulating resources is crucial for high-quality learning to take place. Connections (called synapses) are formed between brain cells (neurons) to make complex neural networks. These connections can be made between anything at any time and are extremely active in young children. In a chemical process that involves electric signals, there is a flow of communication between one neuron to another. If connections are used only infrequently, synaptic pruning takes place, and this happens at a greater rate in children than adults, with the implication being for teachers that knowledge and skills need to be meaningfully applied and repeated, otherwise they are forgotten.

A cross-curricular approach deepens and secures learning by allowing pupils to demonstrate understanding through using transferable knowledge and skills in a variety of contexts. The next chapter looks at how children's natural abilities to learn through asking questions, together with their open-minded attitude towards the visual arts, and their liking to creatively express themselves, has been very effectively harnessed in a number of real-world educational projects.

Part II

The visual arts as a central stimulus across areas of learning

Using the visual arts as a central focus for class discussions on a range of themes can be fruitful and enlightening for both teachers and pupils. These interactions can develop into projects that involve historical investigations, scientific enquiry, creative writing and many other skills that are transferable across subject disciplines. Illustrated through examples of practice, the following chapters show how traditional areas of learning, including Literacy, History, Science and Information and Communication Technology, as well as Art and Design, can be taught through the visual arts in a way that engages and motivates children of all ages and abilities.

Chapter 3

Art and literacy

Even before children can speak, they take pleasure in looking at books with colourful pictures, especially when it means sharing quality time with parents, grandparents or siblings. During these special times, they learn to talk and listen, while also beginning to understand how images and the written word can weave together to form a story.

Children learn to 'read' pictures before they learn to read words. In everyday life, they come across simple pictures in the form of signs. A symbol of an arrow shows which direction to go in. A figure in trousers or a skirt indicates which toilets in a cafe are for men or women. These signs can be understood by young children and are extremely helpful to us all if we are in a country where we do not speak the language.

The visual appeal of graphically designed words makes them easily recognizable to young children. It may seem as though they are 'reading' the name of, say, a super-market that they come across regularly, but instead of sounding out the letters, it is the shapes and colours of the words that they notice and recall. Inside the supermarket, branding with distinctive logos, which marry text and pictures together, inform children and adults what is in each packet, carton, bottle and tin, and posters fill the aisles with photographs of the products on special offer that week. Advertisers know that children, as well as their parents, are consumers and that we are all enticed by delicious-looking food and pictures of happy families enjoying mealtimes, such is the power of the image.

So, from a very early age, the development of children's literacy skills also involves the development of their visual literacy skills. Whether seen together or separately, words and pictures are intrinsic to human communication.

To some extent, the pairing of words and pictures will always tell a narrative, fact or fiction, with sequenced events being described in ways that fuel the imagination. The audience are introduced to places and characters, some that they may never meet normally, and transported mentally to another place and time. Pictures help children to decipher stories and act as prompts for their own storytelling, either expanding on ones they have remembered or for inventing something original. The following extract, taken from Ofsted's 2010 report *Learning: Creative Approaches that Raise Standards*, illustrates this rich relationship between images and words. The Creative Writing and Drama lesson is based on the painting *The Castle of Muiden in Winter* (1658) by Jan Beerstraaten:

> In an outstanding drama lesson with a Reception class, the teacher skilfully led the children as they created their own stories and re-enacted a scene based on the picture. The children's language developed as they became caught up in the 'doom and

gloom', words they used themselves, associated with a dark, threatening castle in a winter scene. The activity gave them great scope to invent their own script, improvise scenes and, following the oral-story-telling techniques they had learnt, to introduce a clear structure to the story they were creating.

As the children recorded their experiences, they turned to their writing as a natural follow-on from the stimulating experiences the role play had initiated. The structures for their stories, many presented diagrammatically with connecting arrows, showed how much they had gained from the lesson and how maturely they had considered the task. The teacher had ensured that pupils felt that their views and opinions were valued. The purpose of the written task was clear to everyone. One pupil pointed out: 'I'm writing an interesting opening for my story but, if I don't make it exciting enough, no-one will read on.'

(Ofsted 2010: 18)

During my time as Head of Schools at the National Gallery, I had the privilege to work alongside some well-known children's authors, journalists and poets, including Jacqueline Wilson (Children's Laureate 2005–7), Kevin Brooks and Malorie Blackman, on a project called Articulate. The aim was to design masterclasses for school pupils about the craft of writing using the national collection of western European paintings (1250–1900) as a source of inspiration. After agreeing to be part of the project, I would invite the writers to meet me in the gallery to give them an informal tour. We would walk from room to room chatting about any paintings that, for whatever reason, they were drawn to.

Degas's *Combing the Hair* (1896) fascinated Jacqueline Wilson. The large red painting, showing a young woman having her hair combed, by what we assume to be her maid, had an impact on Jacqueline because, as she explained to the pupils in her workshop, 'I've always had a thing about hair.'[1]

For me, the hair was the bit that I honed in on most . . . Now, as you can see, I've got very short hair. I had very short hair even as a little girl and I longed for long hair and I begged my mum to let me grow my hair. But way back in those days, mums were fiercer. Or maybe my mum was fiercer, but anyway, she wouldn't let me, and I do actually think she had a point, because when I got to be a teenager and started to do my own thing more, I tried to grow my hair and although it stays sort of reasonably under control when it's very short, when I grow it, it sort of sticks out in weird clumps and won't do what it's supposed to do . . . So I've never really had the lovely luxury of really long hair and I always thought how wonderful it would feel . . . hanging on your back and if you had it in plaits to be able to toss it over your shoulders . . . Whenever people ask me what I wanted to be when I grew up, though, I always knew I wanted to write stories . . . I used to think that I would like to be a hairdresser. I could think of nothing nicer than combing and styling people's hair all day long.

(Transcript extract from Jacqueline Wilson's
Articulate masterclass)

Sharing this highly personal reason for choosing Degas's *Combing the Hair* was really appreciated by the young people in her workshops, who were all 11- and 12-year-old girls from several schools in London. They each clasped copies of Jacqueline's novels in the hope that she would sign them, and waited eagerly to hear some tips on how they might learn to write like her themselves.

The workshops first involved the pupils producing character studies. Jacqueline asked the girls to individually sketch out in words a 'pen portrait' for the two characters in the painting. These were only to be in draft form – nothing too concrete, so that they could be adapted to fit the emerging storylines. Jacqueline talked about how they might think of names for the people and to guess their ages. She also discussed how the objects on the table, and in the rest of the room, might help the students to form the personalities of the people and their backstories, or perhaps the mood of the writing might be affected by the painting's dramatic red colour. Importantly, the interpretations were to be unique to each student. It did not matter what Degas's original intentions were. It was for the pupils to use the image as a starting point for their own creative thoughts. The pupils wrote in the first person and found that ideas came to them very quickly. They were encouraged to talk through these with a peer partner and with Jacqueline herself. Everyone asked lots of questions, helping to make the characters more rounded. People wanted to know more about the sort of childhood the characters had. Did they have children? Were they wealthy?

To inject some jeopardy into the budding plots, Jacqueline then asked pupils to think about who might be looking on to the scene or someone that the characters were particularly concerned about. Someone out of view perhaps, peering through a keyhole, or maybe an absent parent. These three character studies were then taken back to school to flesh out in more detail during English lessons. In subsequent lessons, they were used as preparation materials to write an opening scene for a story. Here are two examples from pupils at Elizabeth Garrett Anderson School:

Mother

Scarlet, velvet cloth hung low from the ceiling on a long gold curtain rail in Andrea's room. Andrea, a 14-year-old redhead, sat patiently on her favourite red chair, wearing her favourite red dress, while Deborah, the hired help, combed it thoroughly while muttering under her breath.

'If mother hears you're not doing my hair properly, she'll sack you straight away', Andrea boasted.

'Your mother, young lady, won't see you for the next month, so don't you try and threaten me.'

Deborah threw the comb on the table with fury and stamped out of the room like a rampaging rhino. She seemed to be angry about something; still muttering and mumbling, she made her way down the hall, slamming Andrea's bedroom door behind her.

The Fatal Bump

3rd December

Dear diary, all the tangles are spoiling my lovely hair. It is long and flaming red, which matches my personality. My temper can rise in a flash. Mother says it's like there's a bomb inside me going tick, tick, tick, tick, and it could go off at any second.

Uncle Jim is coming; don't ask who he is because I don't know, but the way mother goes on about him, you would think he was the king. I'm very worried; mother said that uncle Jim doesn't like long hair. Well tough, because mine isn't coming off.

11th December

Dear diary, there's a bump on my head which is troubling me. It is probably just a spot but it is huge; perhaps it will go away sooner or later.

17th December

Dear diary, oh dear it has been a week now and the bump is still there. Now mother has felt it, she is suspicious . . .

28th December

Dear diary, I am so scared. It's like my life got flipped, turned upside down, I am sitting in a hospital bed just because of a little bump, the nurses won't tell me what is happening or if I am going home. Mother is trying to cheer me up by buying me chocolates and magazines.

29th December

Dear diary, the doctor said he would have to do an operation on my bump. I automatically asked him about my hair; he said that I have got cancer, which means all my hair will fall out. I screamed. I screamed so loud that my throat is still hurting. I feel like a part of me is falling out.

Only schools working below national average literacy levels were selected to join the Articulate project. However, as demonstrated in these two examples, the outcomes were of a very high standard. Several factors enabled this to happen. First, as Dewey (1938: 19) recommends, the structure of the workshops allowed for lots of active participation by the pupils in the development of what was being taught, emphasizing 'the freedom of the learner' (Dewey 1938: 22). Second, the contact between the teacher (Jacqueline) and learner was not one of control, but of guidance (Dewey 1938: 21). And finally, the extremely positive experience helped pupils to understand the basics of the creative process from someone who was well known to them for being a master of her craft. By being a writer that they enjoyed reading, Jacqueline was able to build an instant and mutually respectful relationship with the young people, with her excellent subject content knowledge enabling her to gently talk them through how she generates creative writing ideas, and how these could be adapted by the pupils to help them all make progress in understanding how to go about writing creatively themselves. The American psychologist Jerome Bruner, an advocate of the Reggio approach, describes in his book *The Process of Education* the importance of teaching subject principles and attitudes in a form that is 'accessible to the problem-solving learner by modes of thinking that he already possesses . . . this type of transfer is at the heart of the educational process' (Bruner 1960: ix). He calls 'the continual broadening and deepening of knowledge in terms of basic and general ideas' the objective of a *spiral curriculum* (Bruner 1960: 17). Pupils were fully immersed in what they were doing because they were *being* writers, not just learning about what writers do. They clearly understood what was being asked of them and 'recognized the applicability' of the task to the real world (Bruner 1960: 18). The pupils' self-confidence shines through in their writing because the open-ended nature of the activity gave them the opportunity to write about themes they already knew about. The learning was in the realm of their experience, as Dewey would say. It was meaningful to them, making each piece of writing very personal, possibly cathartic, and, in the case of *The Fatal Bump*, very moving.

Developing empathy and putting these feelings into words was in evidence in the student responses to an unusual painting chosen by novelist Kevin Brooks for his masterclass. Kevin writes books for and about young people, so being part of the Articulate project really appealed to him. He was especially keen that students had a chance to show their work to a wider audience online. He wanted to give them the message not to give up on a dream, as he nearly lost hope of getting his first book, *Martyn Pig*, published, until he came to the attention of Barry Cunningham, the man who bought the Harry Potter series for Bloomsbury Children's Books.

During his workshop, which focused on Pietro Longhi's *Exhibition of a Rhinoceros at Venice* (*c*.1751), Kevin shared the principles behind his creative process, although he admitted that up until that point, he had not really analysed it. He said that he always jotted down in a notepad the first things that came into his head when exposed to something unusual, so concentrating on a painting that was about an unusual event (in this case, one of the first times in Europe anyone had seen a rhinoceros) was particularly appropriate. He asked if the pupils had seen the painting before. There was a resounding 'no'. He asked if they had seen *anything* like it before. The pupils hesitated before agreeing, 'in a zoo'. Kevin continued, what if you had never seen a rhinoceros in a zoo, and you saw this animal in front of you, what would you make of it? And he asked them to quickly write down their first thoughts and then encouraged them to talk about them with a friend. This was the basis for a short story that the pupils worked on during the session and back at school. Kevin thought the start of this one from a 12-year-old pupil at Elizabeth Garrett Anderson School was particularly touching:

The Black Rhino-Thing

There it was. It was just standing there, eating hay. I didn't know what it was. It looked like a cross between a dog, hippo and rhino. It looked like a machine or something. Like its every move was programmed in and it was just a robot from the future.

It looked so sad. I couldn't help but go up to a person in the crowd. Everyone was just standing, laughing and staring at the poor creature. I wondered how so many people could get amusement when a poor and innocent animal looked so weak, sad and ill. It was as if all the happiness had been sucked out of it with a syringe and it wouldn't stop sucking until all the happiness was gone. Every last drop.

Another very successful Articulate masterclass was run by *The Sun* newspaper journalist Brian Flynn. He wanted to make the connection between the words a writer uses to describe events and the colours a painter has on their palette to visually describe what they see or feel. In fact, he told the students in his sessions that in journalism, a 'colour piece' is an eyewitness account that tries to evoke to the reader what it is actually like to be at a scene.

He asked the group to think about how they experience something. Going on to explain that we all experience things through our senses, he shared with the pupils a remarkable event that he saw when he was in New York searching for an apartment to rent. Suddenly, he found himself in a position where he needed to record in words what was happening in front of him so that he could communicate with people who were not there the enormity of the event he was witnessing. And for this, he concentrated on his five senses.

> On September 11, 2001, I was running towards the World Trade Center when it came down. I was in Manhattan . . . and I experienced that. It came down in front of me and I realized I was in the middle of what was arguably the most significant event since the end of World War II. I was there, and my job was purely to describe to people what it was like . . . And what I did, I fell back on this . . . by the side of the road in lower Manhattan I was writing as it happened. And I was writing as the second tower came down.
>
> (Transcript extract from Brian Flynn's
> Articulate masterclass)

He then introduced pupils to a large-scale and very dramatic painting called *The Battle of San Romano* (c.1438–40) by Paolo Uccello. In it, mounted soldiers in heavy armour from Florence and Siena fight with axes and lances, some of these broken on the floor. At the centre is the Florentine leader, Niccolò da Mauruzi da Tolentino, who can be identified by his banner, standing out from the crowd wearing elaborate headgear and riding a white steed.

Brian asked the students to imagine that they were at the battle scene and to describe what they were experiencing through their five senses of sight, smell, taste, touch and sound. He told them to listen to what people might be saying in the painting and to include some dialogue in their report. He also asked them to think carefully about adjectives because these words really add detail – 'colour' – to a piece. Another tip he offered was to try to compare what they are seeing to something else by using similes and metaphor, rather than abstract concepts. For example, 'his lance was as long as a flagpole' rather than, 'his lance was three metres in length'.

The students were visibly excited about using the tricks of the trade, taught to them by a top professional. And again, the written outcomes were of a very high standard. Here are two examples by 12-year-old pupils from St Gregory's School:

A Country at War

A country was torn yesterday as the cities of Florence and Siena began battle. After years of unrest and months of accusations, the war has begun. A war set to break families, friends and countrymen apart. An eyewitness recalled, 'the sky was blood red with the sun shinning a glimmer of hope.'

With horns blowing, drums beating and men calling, the cavalries began their charge. The Florentines were smart, taking out the enemy's archers quickly and effectively.

The ground turned from the green of summer to the red of death. Another eyewitness account told of the brutal slaughtering and the blood-curdling cries of dying men.

The Florentines took a decisive victory. Although outnumbered, the Sienese warriors fought hard and long, taking many Florentines with them. But few can match the Florentine might and Siena will need to look to their politicians to bring this war to an end.

The Fight of Warriors

Blood was spilled last night as the armies of Florence and Siena battled, one on one in the fight of San Ramano. Tolentino, the leader of the victorious Florentine force, led his courageous army into the depths of war.

A witness reported, 'I watched my leader stick his vast razor-sharp sword into the air. As he yelled "attack", my heart filled with fear and hesitation, but my muscles were filled with grit determination.'

Tolentino told me, 'Most people believe that if you are a leader you have to keep your head up, be strong and not have any fear. But last night I was scared.'

The gold-coloured spears shone in the light of the sun as men of courage and with brave hearts broke the barrier of insanity and lunacy as they ran into each other with only one thought in their minds: to kill the person in front of them.

During all the Articulate masterclasses, in addition to the students having a very positive experience, where they were learning skills that were explained in an appropriate way for their level and prior knowledge at that time, and where they were given scope to use their new skills to express their own ideas, their impressive achievements were helped further by the sheer range of skills that were being employed and developed. This meant that pupils who had a preference for using one type of skill over another had the chance to further their strengths in these, while at the same time improving their weaknesses in others. For example, students who were able to confidently verbally demonstrate their observational and analytical skills in a group discussion, but who found writing down their thoughts more difficult, discovered that they were able to express their ideas far better in text after being shown some useful writing exercises based on these discussions. Other pupils, who had a tendency to avoid collaborative open-ended discussions, in this case about a work of art, found that the social interactivity both aided their speaking and listening skills and their ability to be more imaginative in their writing.

For some pupils, the discovery of an untapped or overlooked ability that only comes to light in a positive learning environment that allows it to flourish can mark an important turning point in their general educational performance. It can be the case that some pupils' talents have not been nurtured up to this point because the conditions in which they learn best may not be seen to easily translate to preparing pupils for tests, like standardized testing (SATs). These target-driven assessments measure logical and linguistic skills demonstrated by pupils at speed. They are used to benchmark performances and are a compulsory part of what teachers need to plan for. However, they are blunt instruments and should not dictate an approach to teaching that disengages many pupils from their learning and perpetuates a perception of intelligence that involves only these skills.

Research into describing a broader view of human thought than can be measured by these kinds of tests was undertaken in 1979 by Howard Gardner and a small team at Harvard Graduate School. They began 'with the problems that humans *solve* and worked back to the "intelligences" that must be responsible' (Gardner 1993: 26).

> An intelligence entails the ability to solve problems or fashion products that are of consequence in a particular cultural setting or community. The problem-solving skill allows one to approach a situation in which a goal is to be obtained and to locate the appropriate route to that goal. The creation of a *cultural* product is crucial to such functions as capturing and transmitting knowledge or expressing one's views or feelings. The problems to be solved range from creating an end for a story to anticipating a mating move in chess to repairing a quilt. Products range from scientific theories to musical compositions to successful political campaigns.
>
> (Gardner 1993: 15, original emphasis)

Known as the theory of Multiple Intelligences (MI), the research focused on evidence about development in normal and gifted individuals, studies of exceptional populations, such as prodigies and autistic children, and the breakdown of cognitive skills under conditions of brain damage; this looked at how certain parts of the brain play important roles in intelligent capacities. Originally, seven intelligences were identified: linguistic, logical-mathematical, spatial, bodily-kinaesthetic, musical, inter-personal and intrapersonal. Each had to satisfy strict criteria. For example, they had to be associated with a culturally accepted system of codes that communicate informa-tion, such as language, musical and mathematical notation, and pictorial symbols. Intelligences, even at a basic level in early childhood, can be demonstrated through these symbol systems – language through stories, music through singing, spatial awareness through drawing and bodily-kinesthetic intelligence through dance. Later, more intelligences were considered and added to the list by Gardner, although artistic intelligence was not one of them. He thought that technically:

> no intelligence is inherently artistic or nonartistic. Rather, intelligences function artistically (or nonartistically) . . . should an individual use language in an ordinary way . . . he or she is not using the linguistic intelligence in an aesthetic manner. If, on the other hand, language is used metaphorically, expressively . . . then it is being used artistically . . . By the same token, the same spatial intelligence may be exploited aesthetically by a sculptor, nonartistically by a geometer or surgeon.
>
> (Gardner 1993: 46)

Although Gardner himself said that 'There is no recipe for a multiple intelligence education' (Gardner 1993: 66), as an account of human cognition that has been subjected to empirical tests, MI theory is useful in highlighting why teachers need to offer a variety of opportunities that help pupils to learn in ways that suit their different cognitive capacities, enabling them to find their talents and identify weaknesses that can possibly be improved using 'a secondary route to the solution to the problem' (Gardner 1993: 33).

This simultaneous development of different skills, sometimes with an emphasis on one helping to develop another, was evident in the Articulate masterclasses. It was clear, for example, that where pupils were given time to consider their responses to a painting, and where they were encouraged to expand on their ideas with others, and benefit from professional expertise, many of the MI intelligences were stimulated to some degree, including linguistic and logical-mathematical abilities. In general, observational, analytical, creative, communication and reflective skills are all necessary if a pupil's response to the visual arts is verbal or written, as in the case of the Articulate project. These skills are also needed if the response is transcribed into a piece of dance, a piece of music or another work of visual art.

During the Renaissance, Leonardo da Vinci, famous for his exceptional skills in a range of disciplines, including the arts and sciences, did not suffer from having one of his talents intellectually valued over another. It was the interconnected nature of his talents that enabled his remarkable technical innovation and artistic accomplishment. Similarly, as teachers, by acknowledging the skills that are involved in responding to and making works of art, we can celebrate the interconnectedness between disciplines and help pupils reap the rewards in terms of understanding links, valuing their own abilities, improving their self-confidence and increasing their overall educational performance.

Particularly striking in the outcomes from the Articulate project was the strong emotional response that many pupils felt towards paintings. They can be described as provocative objects (Thornton and Brunton 2009) that serve as excellent resources for developing interpersonal skills (noticing distinctions among other people) and intrapersonal skills (understanding one's own behaviour). This was manifested in different ways. Sometimes, the image would prompt personal memories to come to the fore, which were then used as the starting points for the creative writing, as in *The Fatal Bump*, based on Degas's *Combing the Hair* (1896). For other pupils, it was the empathy that they felt towards a character in a painting that initiated an exploration into expressing mood, such as *The Black Rhino-Thing*, based on Pietro Longhi's *Exhibition of a Rhinoceros at Venice* (*c.*1751).

In a comparable but humorous way, the English poet U.A. Fanthorpe was compelled by the plight of the characters in Paolo Uccello's *Saint George and the Dragon* (*c.*1470). In this first verse, she is speaking in the voice of the two-legged dragon who is being lanced through the nostril by a very young looking Saint George, fearlessly rescuing a rather perplexed princess who is holding the dragon on a leash. The following two verses take on the personalities of first the princess and then George himself. The story is from *The Golden Legend*, the thirteenth-century collection of saints' lives.

Not my Best Side

Not my best side, I'm afraid.
The artist didn't give me a chance to
Pose properly, and as you can see,
Poor chap, he had this obsession with
Triangles, so he left off two of my

Feet. I didn't comment at the time
(What, after all, are two feet
To a monster?) but afterwards
I was sorry for the bad publicity.
Why, I said to myself, should my conqueror
Be so ostentatiously beardless, and ride
A horse with a deformed neck and square hoofs?
Why should my victim be so
Unattractive as to be inedible,
And why should she have me literally
On a string? I don't mind dying
Ritually, since I always rise again,
But I should have liked a little more blood
To show they were taking me seriously.

(Fanthorpe 2010)

Works of art are undoubtedly superb sources of inspiration for writing, speaking and listening activities, role play and drama. More examples of these are illustrated in cross-curricular projects in the next two chapters. Accessing works of art using an open-ended approach rather than, initially at least, from an art historical perspective, emphasizes the involvement of the viewer in the creative process. The visual arts have the power to capture people's imaginations and, in turn, install confidence, because unlike the more passive pursuit of watching a television programme, less fully realized information is offered by the artist, therefore making each person's interpretation unique. Those that it inspires can match the creativity of the visual artist who produced the source of inspiration. Poet Margot Henderson explains this creative process beautifully in her work *Reading Between the Lines*, which describes how we need to use our imaginations when looking at a work of art.

Reading Between the Lines

A picture on a wall
that's all
that's that
but it's not just flat
it's not a matter of fact
there's what's real
and what you feel.
Looking at art
is more than that
it's like a mirror
you can see your life in
it's like a window
are you looking out?
or are you looking in?
It's a fine line
it's a sign of the times

when you draw the line
there are all sorts of symbols in it.
There's the artist's dreams
there's what it means
there's how it seems to you.
Who knows what true?
It takes time to divine
Just like a poem is more than its rhyme.
If you read in between the lines.

(Margot Henderson)[2]

A collaborative study looking at what happens in the brain when a person is thinking creatively was undertaken in 2005 by Paul A. Howard-Jones, Elspeth A. Samuel and Guy Claxton from the Graduate School of Education, University of Bristol, Sarah-Jayne Blackmore from the Institute of Cognitive Neuroscience, University College London, and Ian R. Summers from the Biomedical Physics Group, University of Exeter. In a series of experiments with teacher training students, sets of three words were given to participants who were asked to plan the plot of a story that included these. The students were shown three words on a computer screen and given 10 seconds to generate their story. Some of the words sets were related (for example, 'brush', 'teeth' and 'shine') and others were totally unrelated (for example, 'cow', 'zip' and 'star' being one such set). An added permutation of the experiment was that participants were instructed on the screen, at the same time as being shown the word sets, to either 'Be creative' with their story generation or 'Be uncreative'.

Stories were rated for creativity by an expert independent panel. Results from the initial experiments found that:

> The inclusion of unrelated words in the stories improved the rated creativity of the outcomes. It was also evident, as predicted, that the rated creativity of the outcomes of the stories was influenced by providing a 'Be creative' or 'Be uncreative' objective.
>
> (Howard-Jones *et al.* 2005: 243)

With both the related and unrelated sets of words, divergent connections were made between the words when a 'Be creative' instruction was given. With related words, participants tended to introduce their own context. This creativity was enhanced with unrelated words because the context needed to operate on more than one level. It was also observed that participants found it quite difficult not to think divergently with the unrelated words when asked to 'Be uncreative'. The final experiment, where fMRI (functional magnetic resonance imaging) scans were used, revealed that it is possible to detect 'those regions of the brain that were significantly more active in the creative conditions than in the uncreative conditions' (Howard-Jones *et al.* 2005: 245). The more active areas of the brain were identified as those involved in higher mental reasoning skills, including episodic retrieval (remembering events with their associated emotions), working memory and higher cognitive control.

Although, because the neural networks are so complex, it is wrong to think of any one area as solely responsible for any one task, this evidence could offer insights into why the visual arts when used as a stimulus for writing can help pupils produce the impressive results shown in this chapter. Divergent thinking is triggered by artwork and, when pupils are encouraged to 'Be creative' with the open-ended and non-linear characteristics of the stimulus, it taps into possible previous experiences. By exciting higher mental reasoning skills, the quality of the outcomes is higher and more creative.

Notes

1   Transcripts from extracts of the Articulate project masterclasses and examples of student written outcomes are available at: www.nationalgallery.org.uk/articulate/index.html (accessed 13 September 2013).
2   Margot Henderson wrote this poem specifically for her poetry workshop as part of the Articulate project. It appears on the project website at: www.nationalgallery.org.uk/articulate/projects/mh/mh_poem/mh_poem.html (accessed 13 September 2013).

Chapter 4

Using a single painting as a starting point for cross-curricular learning

This chapter focuses on a scheme called Take One Picture, a nationwide project for primary schools run by the National Gallery. Centred around the simple idea of using a single work of art as a starting point for teaching and learning across the curriculum, each year the gallery challenges primary schools to focus on a featured painting from the collection. The purpose is to promote the visual arts within education and to provide teachers with quality teaching resources and a platform for sharing ideas.

Providing access to the nation's collection of western European paintings (1250–1900) for the education and enjoyment of the widest possible audience is a key objective of the publicly funded gallery,[1] and together with its offer of guided tours, lectures, symposiums and other special projects and events, the Take One Picture scheme enables it to reach out to potential new visitors (both at the gallery and online[2]), including teachers, pupils and their families.

Since Take One Picture began in 1995, it has become something of a phenomenon, acting as a model of best practice for other museums and galleries to emulate (more about that later) and attracting many thousands of teachers to an approach that aligns with creative curriculum design and learning that is tailored to the individual needs of pupils – known as personalized learning.

As former Head of Schools at the National Gallery, I had the privilege and pleasure of curating five exhibitions for the scheme, between 2004 and 2008, with my excellent colleague Jan Young, formerly a gallery lecturer and Initial Teacher Education tutor at Roehampton University. From the hundreds of submissions made by schools every year, from across the UK, we selected children's work to display by visiting many of them and talking to teachers and pupils about their experiences of the scheme.

The first Take One Picture exhibition in 1995[3] came about after Mark Hazzard, a head teacher from Windmill Hill School in Swindon, visited the gallery and returned to school with a teachers' pack based on the fourteenth-century devotional altarpiece known as the *Wilton Diptych* (*c.*1395–9) by an unknown artist. By frequently focusing on a reproduction of the painting (supplied as part of the teachers' pack) in lessons over the period of a school term, pupils studied, alongside their teacher, the content and history of the *Wilton Diptych*, as well as learning how it was made.

Covering subject areas including History, English, Science, Design Technology and Religious Education, as well as Art and Design, they learnt about the life of Richard II, King of England from 1377 to 1399; they investigated the stories of the saints depicted standing next to him; they found out about heraldry; experimented with making their own primary colour pigments; mixed egg tempera paint (see page 71 for a recipe);

and, among many other things, practised the art of gilding – a technique used to apply gold leaf to prepared wooden panels, giving an animated appearance to the figures when candlelight is reflected off them.

The pupils' reaction to these rich experiences were so positive that Mark Hazzard contacted the National Gallery's Education department and it was decided to arrange for the work to be displayed in the Education Centre at the gallery as an example of how children's learning can be stimulated by one work of art, fulfilling many requirements of the mandatory National Curriculum in a range of subject areas.

Since then, every year, a painting from the gallery's collection has been chosen for a nationwide primary school challenge, and a physical exhibition celebrating learning outcomes based on the single work of art has been mounted in London, sometimes in the gallery's Education Centre or basement exhibition spaces, other times in more prominent positions in the gallery so a greater number of people have the chance of encountering it. The number of schools having their work selected to be physically displayed varies each year. In the early years, it was between five and 10 schools. The record so far has been 25 schools in 2013. In addition to the physical exhibitions, a dedicated area on the gallery's website showcases all the featured paintings alongside the exhibits dating back to 2001.

In this case study, I am going to concentrate on two of the exhibitions: starting with Degas's nineteenth-century *Beach Scene* (*c*.1868–77), a well-known Impressionist painting, and followed by the Dutch seventeenth-century painting of *Two Boys and a Girl Making Music* (1629) by Jan Molenaer, perhaps less well known but equally as compelling for children and teachers alike.

The seaside is a popular theme for learning across the curriculum in primary schools because links can easily be made between Science and History, at the same time as teaching Literacy and Art and Design. It can also build on pupils' experiences of family holidays and day trips. However, some teachers that I spoke to when visiting schools to select work for the Degas's *Beach Scene* exhibition were surprised by how many children in their class had not yet had the chance to play on a real beach. These schools arranged journeys to their nearest resorts, knowing that first-hand experiences would be crucial to understanding Degas's picture in any depth.

The painting shows a girl lazily lying on the sand. She is having her hair combed by a woman, a motif, as we have already seen in the Articulate project that Degas was keen on. Unlike his artist friends Edouard Manet and Berthe Morisot, who were painting beach scenes at the time *en plein air* (outside), Degas preferred to produce his pictures in a studio. A clue to this is on the horizon where two ships have smoke billowing in opposite directions – something of a joke by the artist to see if we are looking closely enough at his work. Some children are convinced that they can see a shark's fin among the waves, although I hope not as families are splashing in the water!

Adding to the hot holiday mood of the scene, other figures are strolling along the sand wrapped in large white towels, and a swimming costume in the foreground, with long legs and a high neck, belonging to the girl having her hair combed, is neatly laid out to dry in the sun. The costume's style helps us to date the painting, as does the length of the dresses worn by the women. It is clear that covering up was the appropriate way to behave while on the beach in nineteenth-century France.

So, what did pupils and their teachers learn when using this painting as a central stimulus in a cross-curricular project?

As we have already explored, paintings are great resources for prompting creative writing. This is particularly true when the subject matter is in the realm of the pupils' own experiences, as is evident from the use of descriptive language in these two pieces of writing by 7-year-olds from Wisborough Green Primary School in West Sussex. Pupils looked at the use of metaphor and called to mind memories of being at the seaside.

On the Beach

Smelling seawater like salt on chips
Crashing waves along the beach
Breezy wind being pushed away
Seagulls talking like mad
Dribbly babies on the sand
Seaweed pink and green
Sand like sprinkled sugar
Sea tossing and turning
Like dancers swirling
Waves splashing and roaring

Over My Toes

I was on the beach
And a dog scared me out of my skin
I was having a good time,
Until then.
He was all wet and I was eating
Sand and water shaken all over me
I had a swim
It was nice and cool
I felt the water flowing over my toes
I felt seaweed washing over my feet
I came back and shook water all over that dog.

At St Luke's Primary School, Kingston upon Thames, as part of a whole-school project based on the *Beach Scene*, Foundation children (aged 3 to 5 years) were encouraged to look at the objects in the painting and then to bring in items from home that related to them or were similar in colour. These were then woven into a huge real fishing net that was hung across the assembly hall ceiling (Figure 4.1). Discussions took place in both the classroom and at home with family members, helping to bridge the gap between home and school life. Being involved in this way over a sustained period of time enabled children to develop their skills of observation and extend their vocabulary. The exercise also served as a meaningful and colourful way to connect the youngest children to the rest of the school, acting as an instrument for whole-school cohesion.

The youngest pupils at St Mary's School in Bodmin collected driftwood from a beach 10 miles away and with it made beautiful toy sailing boats (Figure 4.2). They were taught how to do this by a parent who was a professional carpenter. When finished, the boats were used by the pupils for a science-based floating and sinking exercise. As part of the same project, the pupils had access to a large role-play boat (named the

Figure 4.1 Foundation stage pupils at St Luke's Primary School, Kingston upon Thames, looked carefully at Degas's *Beach Scene* and then collected items relating to it to weave into a fishing net. The activity developed observation skills and speaking and listening skills, as well as maths skills with sorting and positioning sizes and shapes. Photo: © The National Gallery, London.

'Edgar Degas'), made from an indoor climbing frame and covered in thick cardboard that the children helped to paint. The boat had an upper and lower deck, complete with steering wheel, logbook and 'communication system' (a piece of plastic piping between in top and bottom brackets). This allowed children to relay instructions to each other on matters of navigation, warning about oncoming boats or icebergs they might have spotted in the sea through a telescope. Lifejackets were also provided for the children to wear. These prompted discussions about health and safety, in particular about the importance of learning to swim.

Annotated drawings and accurate three-dimensional models were made by several schools of seaside creatures found in rock pools (Figure 4.3). They studied habitats and environmental issues at the same time as perfecting drawing, modelling and measuring skills.

Research into how the growth of the railways made beach holidays accessible to more people in the nineteenth century informed wider historical investigations. Some schools made enquiries into the history of their local seaside towns, finding photographs and other evidence to build a picture of what these would have been like during the same era as Degas's *Beach Scene*, concentrating on Victorian fashions, events and attitudes.

Pupils at Kew College, London, compared the past and the present in the form of a drama tableau based on the original painting, which they filmed on a real beach. Some pupils acted out the roles of people in the *Beach Scene* and others imagined what the same people would be doing today. Many key skills were developed as a result.

Figure 4.2 Nursery-aged children at St Mary's School, Bodmin, collected driftwood from a beach to make their own model boats, helped by a local carpenter. They then tried to float these in a science-based activity. Photo: © The National Gallery, London.

Costumes were made, filming techniques were learnt, scripts were written and, finally, audiences were presented to.

The focus of the 2007 exhibition was Jan Molenaer's *Two Boys and a Girl Making Music*. It shows three seventeenth-century Dutch children playing a variety of musical instruments, some of which they have made themselves. The image is full of noise and appeals to a viewer's sense of hearing and vision. Musical pictures were a popular theme with painters at the time as a way of exploring ideas about harmony and unity. One of the boys has a violin, while the other has a rommelpot. This was made from a jug containing water with a skin stretched over the top and a stick piercing through it. The resulting noise, when the stick was moved up and down, would have been quite loud and rude sounding – and therefore, of course, very amusing to children! The girl in the middle of the picture, wearing part of a suit of armour around her neck, is also making a loud noise by banging a metal helmet with spoons like a drum. Other objects in the picture relating to the military, such as the folding chair, on which one of the boys sits, and a large trunk in the corner of the dark room, probably refer to the Thirty Years War, a religious and political conflict that engulfed central Europe in the early seventeenth century.

Many children comment on how the characters in the picture look poor because their shoes have holes in them and their clothes are mismatched. Others think that a dressing-up game is taking place, with more costumes stored in the trunk. What is clear is that whoever the children in the painting are and whatever they are doing, lots of fun is being had, and this is very much something that twenty-first-century children can relate to. Although hundreds of years apart from the children in the painting, the children looking at them from outside of the frame enjoy the same things, and this fact means that the painting makes sense to them.

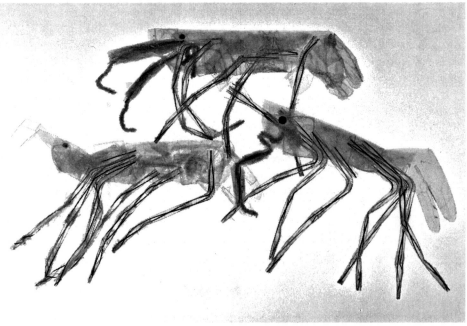

Figure 4.3 Pupils from Dorridge Junior School, Solihull, made scientific investigations into creatures that can be found in seaside habitats. Photo: © The National Gallery, London.

The piece can be viewed as a celebration of childhood, but it is also a gentle reminder that this period of a person's life is short-lived. In the form of an empty birdcage a symbol of transience sits on the floor, telling us that sooner or later these young people will 'fly the nest' to become adults, and perhaps have children of their own, a visual message that gives rise to discussions in the classroom about growing up, families and relationships.

Seven schools were selected to show their work in the *Two Boys and a Girl Making Music* Take One Picture exhibition, with over 43,000 children, teachers and non-teaching staff involved in making formal submissions to the scheme that year. Highlights included the poem below, co-written by three Year 4 pupils (8- and 9-year-olds) from Wentworth CE Junior and Infant School, Rotherham, a school that later became an integral part of a regional visual arts education scheme called Picture This!, introduced in the next chapter:

Three Friends

We are three friends and we all stick together,
Playing music and dancing forever and ever.
We love entertaining, dancing in the streets,
Getting money for food so we can all eat.
We love being friends,
We like it a lot,
We also love playing,
With that big rommelpot.

Other notable ideas from schools based on the painting included the making of instruments from recycled materials, which helped to develop knowledge, skills and understanding in Music, Design Technology, Art and Design, and Science. After investigating various musical instruments from first-hand experience, pupils constructed their own working models. They experimented with sound, shape, scale and different materials, including wood, card, metal, wire, string and elastic bands. Recording the design process in writing, and also using digital photography, assisted the pupils' evaluations.

Hundreds of rommelpots were made across the country as part of Science, Design Technology and Music lessons. Plastic cups, yogurt pots and glass jars were all tested to see how they worked with either rubber gloves, balloons or waxed paper stretched over the top. Varying levels of water were used to produce different pitches. At Wentworth CE Junior and Infant School, some children in an extended hours after-school club made authentic ceramic rommelpots (Figure 4.4), coiling their own clay vessels and using real deer skin over the top – which went mouldy!

Animations were also very popular. At one school, pupils learnt about possible careers in an animation studio. They wrote the job descriptions and even applied for the position that they wanted to take on during the project. This enterprising approach allowed them to play to their strengths, using preferred learning skills while working as part of a team. A whole mixed class of Year 4, 5 and 6 pupils (between 8 and 11 years old) at Horningsham School, Wiltshire, generated ideas for a script inspired by the painting in collaboration with a local children's author and illustrator. They made characters

Figure 4.4 Authentic rommelpots were made by pupils in art club at Wentworth CE Junior and Infant School, Rotherham. Photo: © The National Gallery, London.

and props from modelling clay (Figure 4.5) and built a set that they then used to produce an animated digital film. They composed a soundtrack for the film by listening to Dutch seventeenth-century music and writing their own musical phrases. At the end of the project, the pupils advertised a premiere performance of the film to parents and the local community, raising money for charity at the event.

The longevity of the Take One Picture project offers valuable insights into using the visual arts in primary education for cross-curricular teaching and learning for teachers and museum and gallery educators. Dialogue in the form of the submissions from schools, conversations during school visits, audience feedback from exhibitions and presentations made by teachers and gallery educators at regular teachers' courses, has meant that the rationales and strategies for using paintings in the classroom have been shared.

Over the years, a number of independent evaluations of Take One Picture have also been commissioned. In 2005–6, Alix Slater, Principal Lecturer in Cultural Industries Management at the University of Greenwich Business School, sent 150 questionnaires to 180 schools submitting work for the *Two Boys and a Girl Making Music* exhibition and undertook 30 interviews, conducted during school visits. Of the 57 per cent of teachers who responded to the questionnaires, 92 per cent believed that the approach

Figure 4.5 A mixed class of 8- to 11-year-olds from Horningsham Primary School, Wiltshire, worked with a local author/illustrator to create an animation based on Molenaer's *Two Boys and a Girl Making Music*. Photo: © The National Gallery, London.

improved their pupils' learning and performance, 90 per cent said that it enhanced children's ability to work together in groups, and 87 per cent said that it increased communication skills. Qualitative responses to open questions that focused on teachers' expectations before and after undertaking a Take One Picture project (for example, a question about whether Take One Picture had changed their approach to planning and delivering the curriculum) included:

> It was a different way of working for most staff and working together raised standards.
>
> (Head Teacher, Hertfordshire)

> It provides a real context for discussing and presenting ideas. It gives children a passion for art, and really exciting and creative opportunities for learning . . . The children can really get into the characters and compare themselves with who is in the painting. If you capture children's imaginations, then that's a gift.
>
> (Head Teacher, Wiltshire)

> The process has been invaluable to our staff, parents and children.
>
> (Head Teacher, West Yorkshire)

> As educators, we enjoy learning too, and it is amazing the learning journey that is undertaken from one piece of art.
>
> (Science, Art and Drama Coordinator, Hampshire)

> I think the greatest plus of doing something like this is that nothing is wrong. Nobody is going to wag a finger and say, 'you can't say that' or, 'you shouldn't be writing that' because their [the children's] interpretation is from within.'
>
> (Classroom Teacher, Bognor Regis)

There is a serious need to bring back creativity, and Take One Picture achieves this.

(Deputy Head Teacher, Norfolk)

Children talked more to each other about their work and had opportunities to work with peers from other classes … parents were encouraged to visit the National Gallery, and many did.

(Head Teacher, London)

It's a fantastic way of developing imagination.

(Deputy Head Teacher, Hertfordshire)

Using Take One Picture as the basis for a whole-school project has a tremendous impact on school ethos. There was a real feeling of 'oneness' and shared unity between all staff and pupils. There was a wonderful sense of sharing and appreciation of the work produced by every single child in the school.

(Art Coordinator, Surrey)

It's not often that children will just sit down and have time and space to look at a picture. The children are stimulated by it. They are in a more heightened state of emotion, which is when they remember things.

(Head Teacher, Dorset)

It's been lovely having a common theme from Reception to Year 6.

(Deputy Head Teacher, Dorset)

The evaluation concluded:

Although respondents' expectations of Take One Picture are high, in some ways they are still exceeded, especially at a school level. Not surprisingly as teachers get more experienced they see the wider benefits of Take One Picture and are then more likely to share good practice beyond their own institution.

Prompted by the enthusiasm of the participating schools, and particularly by the notion that schools who repeatedly use the Take One Picture approach see 'wider benefits', I invited five schools[4] that had regularly made submissions to the scheme to join a research project, with the view of understanding more deeply the complex nature of using works of art as a focus for teaching and learning.

Involving 25 teachers, five from each school, the research followed a case study model as the teachers were working in real-life contexts without any restrictions on their behaviour being put into place. The data was collected between autumn 2007 and autumn 2008 using three methods – written surveys, log journals and semi-structured interviews – the triangulation of which improved the reliability of the findings. Written surveys were designed to allow the teachers to articulate their rationale. Log journals were treated as personal professional diaries where teachers could record an overview of the lessons being taught, including prior planning needed, teaching strategies, equipment used, any additional support required, expected learning outcomes and actual learning outcomes (if different), as well as specific pupil reactions (using descriptions and quotes) with examples of children's work. Semi-structured interviews enabled me to track the teachers' thought processes from the project planning stage to implementation. My questions particularly explored pupils' and teachers' reactions to the approach; what, if any, evidence was there of progression in children's learning; in which subjects; which key skills were developed; and comments on organizational aspects (for example, what the motivation was for schools and individual teachers to use artwork for cross-curricular teaching and learning). Analytical generalizations were made from the descriptive answers, first by coding them into clusters and then grouping emerging themes.

Five common trends became evident, helping to characterize the nature of using paintings for teaching and learning across the curriculum. They crystallize why the visual arts are such a powerful stimulus in an educational setting and dovetail with the educational theories and real-life practices that I have described in previous chapters that centre on nurturing the child as an individual.

Trend 1: allowing for learning to be personalized

First, using a painting as a central stimulus allows teachers flexibility to personalize learning, where pupils have opportunities to steer their own learning by expressing their own thoughts and ideas and setting lines of enquiry. This means that projects can be designed around pupils' interests, building on prior knowledge, and therefore making learning more engaging. Teachers also can help children to develop their talents and identify and improve skills that are weaker. This aligns with EYFS (Early Years Foundation Stage) principles, briefly outlined in Part I, a framework that encourages personal exploration and sustained shared thinking. Many teachers believe that pupils at KS 1 and KS 2, and higher, would benefit from the continuation of this approach throughout their school careers. There is much evidence in this book to support this view, as well as the findings of the 2012 report by Ofsted, *Making a Mark: Art, Craft and Design Education 2008–11*:

> Teaching was more effective in the early years and post-16 because there was a greater emphasis on personalization ... In all phases of education, pupils' and students' spiritual, moral, social and cultural development grew through topics that embraced their personal interests and experience.
>
> (Ofsted 2012a: 7)

Trend 2: promoting first-hand experiences

Second, the experiential approach that Take One Picture promotes gives pupils opportunities for creative learning using a number of first-hand experiences. This makes learning more meaningful and leads to improved educational performance through the development of transferable key skills (discussed in Part III) (for example, speaking and listening and writing skills).

Trend 3: interrelating essential knowledge, key concepts and skills across subject areas

Third, learning is made more meaningful by demonstrating how essential knowledge (also discussed in Part III) and key concepts and skills are interrelated across groups of subject areas. Pupils are also given the chance to show their understanding of these links.

Trend 4: improving whole-school and community cohesion

Fourth, sharing a stimulus with other year groups as a starting point for projects that can be accessed by different levels of ability and that meet the statutory requirements for EYFS and KS 1 and KS 2 enables schools to structure learning in ways that can improve whole-school and community cohesion. A head teacher once told me how she had overheard two boys walking out of the toilets at break time, one from Year 1 and the other from Year 6, chatting about Molenaer's *Two Boys and a Girl Making Music* painting. For her, this was clear evidence that a whole-school focus around a single work of art was extremely worthwhile. A single focus can also benefit out-of-school and family learning projects. Ofsted highlighted the relationship between home and school as being underdeveloped in many schools (Ofsted 2012a: 7), where a lack of information and guidance resulted in pupils missing opportunities to extend their interests and talents in their leisure time. This could effectively be addressed through projects that encourage reciprocal links between the classroom and a child's family environment through the continuation of a theme, acknowledging and advancing further the major impact that parents and carers have on shaping a child's image of him or herself as a learner (Alexander 2010: 82).

Trend 5: nurturing teachers' interests as well as pupils'

Finally, as the stimulus is usually unfamiliar to the teachers, they need to learn about subjects and techniques alongside their pupils, sharing ideas with colleagues and sometimes also harnessing the relevant talents of parents and governors, and making partnerships with outside organizations. Most of the teachers who took part in the research project said that they very much welcomed this aspect of Take One Picture and described how it had reawakened an old, and sometimes ignited a new, interest in art, galleries and museums. This not only improved their teaching because they were genuinely excited by the content of their lessons, but they were also modelling good behaviour as learners themselves.

The head teachers at all the five research schools placed particular emphasis on this fifth trend. In their written surveys and interviews, a personal enthusiasm for the visual arts was cited as a motivating factor for joining in with Take One Picture. They expressed a desire to impart this personal enthusiasm to their staff via the scheme, many of whom had had little visual arts training during their Initial Teacher Education (ITE) courses, as well as to their pupils.

I have always been positive about the value of art both on a personal and professional level. I enjoy visiting art galleries and creative hobbies like sewing, embroidery, and crafts in general.

(Head Teacher, Rotherham)

I am very interested in looking at art and visit galleries a lot. I have collected some pieces, mainly ceramics.

(Head Teacher, Nottingham)

I have been engaged in art all my life – both the visual and the performance arts. My father was assistant director/curator of the Walters Art Gallery, Baltimore, Maryland . . . I was exposed to and included in many activities that were centred on the arts. The involvement has continued all my life and I want the same for the pupils in my care.

(Head Teacher, Wolverhampton)

I enjoy looking at art and visiting exhibitions.

(Head Teacher, Northampton)

I have always had an interest in art through parents who took me to galleries when I was young and good teaching. I have no qualifications in Art but studied English and Music at university, which maintained and developed my interest in the arts. I am married to a professional artist and my daughter is a children's book designer and illustrator, so I am surrounded by art at home! I was a guide for many years at Wightwick Manor, a National Trust property with an excellent collection of pre-Raphaelite paintings and Arts and Crafts furniture.

(Head Teacher, Wolverhampton)

Because of their interest in the arts, the head teachers were able to articulate and evaluate the contribution that the visual arts have on the creative and cultural development of their pupils, and they wholeheartedly support their staff in providing a curriculum that imaginatively involves the visual arts in a range of curriculum subjects. To what extent their staff are able to achieve these ambitions depends as much on their confidence with cross-curricular planning as it does on their subject-content knowledge and pedagogical-content knowledge of Art and Design, History, Science and other subjects. Because within the schools there is already a great deal of expertise in creative cross-curricular teaching and learning, due to the head teachers' interests and employing other staff that are sympathetic to their own creative ideas, there is a high level of assistance from colleagues and Continuing Professional Development (CPD) input is regular.

This is not always the case in schools where the leadership is less convinced by the value of the visual arts for cross-subject learning. A 2003 survey of the arts in primary schools in England by the National Foundation for Educational Research (Downing *et al.* 2003) recognized that recruiting generalist teaching staff with specialisms in literacy and numeracy is the main concern of many schools and that this can be to the detriment of pupils' learning experiences in the arts:

The priority for head teachers in recruiting staff is to have all-rounders who can cope with the whole curriculum, with literacy and numeracy taking precedence. Given that most class teachers have not specialized in an art form in their ITT [Initial Teacher Training], it is inevitable that most will be teaching some arts subjects for which they were not initially trained. Although some have addressed this with CPD in the arts and others are supported by arts specialists within their schools, it is not surprising that many express a shortfall of confidence in teaching the arts. This may be more acute in the arts than in other areas of the curriculum, as many people find expression in the arts personally challenging or even embarrassing.

(Downing *et al.* 2003: 31)

Concerns were voiced at the National Gallery Take One Picture Annual Conference in 2002 about not only the deficiency in arts training that teachers new to the profession seemed to have, but also their lack of cross-curricular planning experience. Head teachers raised the issue that Newly Qualified Teachers (NQTs) were very competent at teaching the numeracy and literacy strategies, but often not so aware of creative curriculum planning. An increased focus at the time on student teachers using published schemes of work (for example, those produced by the Qualifications and Curriculum Development Agency, or QCA), rather than concentrating on the ingredients that are important to plan effectively for learning, meant that many were completing their initial training without an adequate grounding in designing their own lessons around the specific needs of the children that they teach. Although sometimes useful for non-subject specialists, published schemes of work, if not at least adapted to meet the needs and interests of the pupils being taught, can be restrictive and overly prescriptive. Teachers using these resources also tend to be more removed from the learning process, as they have not invested their own interests, knowledge and skills into the planning. In general, the view of experienced teachers is that creativity is synonymous with teaching. If the creative process of planning and shaping the context for learning and learning objectives around the pupils is removed, then the professional judgement and practice of teachers is undermined.

In response to these concerns, a Cultural Placement Partnership Programme was set up at the National Gallery for trainee teachers, first with Roehampton University, and in subsequent years this was expanded to five other universities, Oxford Brookes, Edge Hill, Nottingham Trent, Leeds Metropolitan and East Anglia. The programme offered ITE students the chance to immerse themselves in finding out about how the visual arts can be effectively used for cross-curricular teaching and learning and to experience teaching for themselves in 'a setting other than a school' (known as SOTS), in accordance with recommendations in the newly published professional standards at the time (Training and Development Agency for Schools 2002).

On a structured formal basis, the National Gallery started to welcome ITE students on week-long placements where they were able to observe professional teaching practice in a non-classroom setting,[5] particularly concentrating on pupil-teacher interactions, including questioning techniques and scaffolding understanding. They learnt through Take One Picture-based workshops how to plan cross-curricular lessons and projects using cultural objects to inspire, and on the final day they had the opportunity to teach a group of pupils in front of an original work of art in a public gallery.

The cultural placements enabled ITE students to observe and demonstrate how to:

- encourage children to use their prior knowledge to access a painting;
- improve pupils' questioning and skills of investigation by asking open-ended questions about what they can see (for example, what they think might be happening, when it might be happening and so forth);
- feed pupils' imaginations by looking at what might be implied in a work of art through symbolic references;
- encourage pupils to 'wander off' into a landscape, exploring what they find and comparing it to what they already know;
- use paintings as historical evidence, investigating the authenticity of items, including costume, and considering the cultural attitudes and customs of the time; and
- help pupils to set their own lines of enquiry by suggesting where they can find out more information about what they are interested in, and how this might link with other learning.

Pivotal to the sustainability of the programme was the brokering of relationships between the students' universities and partner schools, and their regional museums and galleries. With government funding,[6] students were able to access printed and digital reproductions of selected paintings from collections local to them, along with teachers' notes written by education staff from the regional museums and galleries. They used these in designing their own Take One Picture-style projects to teach on their school experience placements. Many ITE students arranged class visits to their local collections; they collaborated in mounting exhibitions of children's work at their universities and local museums and galleries; attended private views with pupils, parents and staff from their placement schools and universities; and produced resources to use in the next stage of their teaching careers.

The programme was a huge success, with over 900 ITE students to date undertaking a cultural placement in London or with an associate partner organization.[7] Comments from end-of-placement evaluations in autumn 2006 included:

I was overwhelmed by the wealth of cross-curricular links that could be created by one image.

(ITE Student, Roehampton University)

I have come away with such a mountain of useful information, strategies and confidence! I've decided to make a portfolio of my experience and I can't wait to show and share my ideas in my new school placement.

(ITE Student, Roehampton University)

I had a fantastic time. I learnt more than I thought possible in one week ... I'm really looking forward to implementing the ideas we explored in my classroom, and subsequently into my final year dissertation. I feel really fired up and enthusiastic about it. Thanks!

(ITE Student, Oxford Brookes University)

Dr Julie Shaughnessy, Principle Lecturer in Education at Roehampton University, said:

> Through the Take One Picture approach, ITE students are encouraged to use the visual arts as a vehicle for learning across the curriculum . . . this also connects to deepening ITE students' engagement beyond the immediate image and reflect on the learning process.

Dr Tony Cotton, Principle Lecturer in Primary Education at the time at Nottingham Trent University, said:

> The appropriateness of the pedagogy which is modelled through the Take One Picture approach is highly relevant, in particular the emphasis which is placed on probing questions to elicit children's own understanding and the careful scaffolding of learning after initially exploring children's own starting points.

Dr Jennie McFadden, ITE Programme Leader at the time at Oxford Brookes University, said:

> The project has greatly enriched students' training and, in enabling them to teach in a setting outside the classroom, has added a new dimension to their experience.

Two independent studies were made of the Cultural Placement Partnership Programme. On behalf of the Department for Culture Media and Sport (DCMS) and the Department for Children, Schools and Families (DCSF), who jointly funded the project as part of a larger programme called Strategic Commissioning: National/ Regional Museum Education Partnerships, the Research Centre for Museums and Galleries, based at the University of Leicester, highlighted how 'there was as great a deal of satisfaction with how the project had been developed and the learning outcomes it enabled, not just for pupils but also for ITE students and also teachers' (RCMG 2007: 26). Dominic Wyse and Laura McGarty from the University of Cambridge Faculty of Education were commissioned by the National Gallery to evaluate the overall impact of the Cultural Placement Partnership in 2009. They reported 'A remarkable level of excitement about the use of paintings to support innovative teaching was evident from almost all of the participants in the National Gallery Initial Teacher Education Cultural Placement Partnership.' Very importantly, there was also 'evidence that pedagogical risk-taking was positively changing the ideas not only of the trainees themselves but also of experienced teachers with whom the trainees were working' (Wyse and McGarty 2009: 3). Where experienced teachers had been critical of the ability of teachers new to the profession to think and plan creatively, now it was the ITE students injecting new ways of working into schools.

The legacy of Take One Picture has been extensive. Through the ongoing nationwide scheme, hundreds of primary schools each year are either introduced to or continue to use the holistic cross-curricular approach. In recent years, the National Gallery has started using the idea with selected secondary schools, in a project named Picture in Focus, and according to an independent evaluation, again by Dominic Wyse and Laura McGarty at the University of Cambridge Faculty of Education, 'There was ample evidence from the data of perceptions that learning had been significantly enriched by the project' and 'The depth of learning reported when different subjects are combined around a common stimulus to provide a holistic perspective was noted by both teachers and their pupils' (Wyse and McGarty 2010: 21). The Take One Picture scheme has also influenced other museums and galleries across the UK and beyond to launch their own similar projects. Some of these have been linked to the Cultural Placement Partnership Programme. For example, Nottingham City Museums and Galleries and the Ashmolean Museum of Art and Archaeology, in Oxford, both now run regional cross-curricular projects with local primary schools, and Oxford Brookes University offers modules for ITE students designed around the benefits of cultural placements. Other museums and galleries have adapted the concept of using a single work of art as a stimulus for learning across the curriculum to suit their own collections after learning about the approach from local teachers who have taken part in the national scheme. Northampton Museum and Art Gallery, which houses the world's largest collection of boots and shoes, has a Take One Shoe project. And in Rotherham, the council school effectiveness service have set up a programme called Picture This!, involving schools from across their borough in a huge annual visual arts project, examined in more detail in the next chapter.

Notes

1   'The key objectives of the Gallery are to promote education and knowledge about the paintings; to study them; to add great paintings to the collection; and to keep them safe for present and future generations' (National Gallery 2007: 4).
2   www.takeonepicture.org/ (accessed 30 October 2013).
3   The exhibition was shown in the Education Centre at the National Gallery, 18 November 1995–7 January 1996.
4   Castlecroft Primary School, Wolverhampton, East Park Infant School, Wolverhampton, Flore Church of England Primary School, Northampton, Maun Infant and Nursery School, Nottingham, Wentworth Junior and Infant School, Rotherham.
5   On average, 80,000 school children per year aged between 3 and 18 years have interactive guided tours of the National Gallery, looking at between three to five paintings in an hour on a curriculum-linked theme.
6   Between 2003 and 2010, the Department for Culture Media and Sport (DCMS) and the Department for Education and Skills (DfES)/Department for Children, Schools and Families (DCSF) jointly funded partnerships between national and regional museums in England with the aim of increasing and deepening relationships between museums, galleries, and schools and communities. The programme was called Strategic Commissioning: National/Regional Museum Education Partnerships.
7   Associate partner organizations include the Ashmolean Museum of Art and Archeology, Oxford; the Walker Gallery, Liverpool; Nottingham Castle Museum and Art Gallery; Leeds Art Gallery; and Norwich Castle Museum and Art Gallery.

Chapter 5

Keeping it local

Discovering the wealth of art resources in your region and using them to learn about local history

A school project that centres on a work of art of local significance can encompass a large number of subject-specific learning objectives. As well as Art and Design objectives, including investigating different kinds of art, craft and design from a range of cultures and periods in the context in which the work was made, learning objectives for the humanities can be taught (for example, analysing artefacts, retelling stories from history, placing objects and events in chronological order and considering why people in the past acted as they did). By providing pupils with a starting point, where they can use their own prior knowledge of the place in which they live, they can compare this information with what they find out. A project such as this can heighten the interest of the school's wider community in the work of the pupils and teachers through members of the public helping in the process of discovery, and also through them attending physical exhibitions, or other celebrations, that present the pupils' findings and responses.

The art focus could be an important piece of jewellery or item of ceramics found in a nearby archaeological dig and displayed in a local museum. Or perhaps an ancient map, showing recognizable locations. A piece of textiles by a local craftsperson, either from the past or contemporary, would make a fascinating study, as would a painting depicting a traditional event, or portrait of a local hero, or a piece of public art, such as a statue. They would all act as excellent stimuli for cross-curricular explorations that have a special relevance to children, their teachers and families from a specific place.

As part of an extension of the National Gallery's Take One Picture scheme, Nottingham City Museums and Galleries have encouraged many schools across their county to study works of art depicting people and events of regional interest held in local collections. These have included the paintings *Robin Hood and his Merry Men Entertaining Richard the Lionheart in Sherwood Forest* (1839) by Daniel Maclise, *Nottingham from the East* (1695) by Jan Siberechts, and *The Goose Fair, Nottingham* (1926) by Arthur Spooner. Pupil outcomes from studying these have been displayed at culture centres in the city and on a specially dedicated section of a website called Museum Buddies, which aims to connect museum and gallery audiences in the East Midlands through digital projects.[1]

On the Northamptonshire–Warwickshire border, a school that had been chosen to show their work in the Take One Picture exhibition several times decided to look closer to home for inspiration for their annual whole-school visual arts project. All the pupils at Flore CE Primary looked at a work of art depicting a local place by a local artist on display at Leamington Spa Art Gallery and Museum. Picturing a serene landscape within

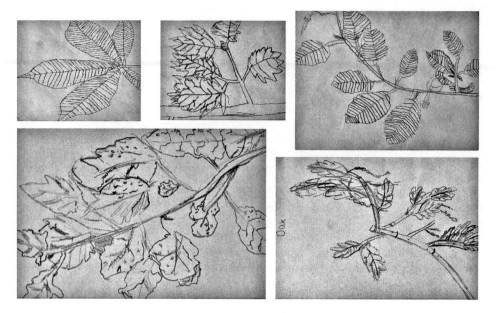

Figure 5.1 First-hand observational drawing develops pupils' scientific investigation skills.

parkland not far from the school, *The Leam near Willes Road Bridge, Warwickshire* (*c*.1880) by Frederick Whitehead enthused every year group to undertake cross-curricular work.

A visit to the beauty spot where the artist had originally set up his easel to produce the painting helped teachers to gauge their pupils' interests in possible directions for sustained enquiries. It was also the setting for pre-planned activities. For KS 2 pupils, these directed tasks included starting to investigate the life cycle of green plants through accurate first-hand observational pencil drawings of different leaf specimens (Figure 5.1), leading to a joint Art and Design and Science-based lesson on classification and learning about the different parts of plants when they got back to the classroom. Geography fieldwork linked to the theme of rivers took place in the park, where pupils followed the course of the River Leam, seen in the painting, recording it through digital photography. The much longer River Nene that rises in their home county was the subject of a similar activity by another class on return to school.

Some students wanted to find out more about landscape gardening after a chance meeting with the head gardener while he planted flowerbeds. Teachers linked this interest to a Maths activity learning about pattern and symmetry. For a Design Technology project, photographs were taken of botanical architectural structures in the park. These were used to generate ideas back at school for modern park shelters, thinking particularly about the needs of different groups of people who frequently use the public space.

Younger pupils spent time drawing statues of elephants that they found in the grounds of the park, learning from their teachers that these were there because the world-famous Victorian animal trainer Sam Lockhart allowed his elephants to bathe in the River Leam. Following up this true story back in the classroom, the pupils later read *Elephants in*

Royal Leamington Spa by Janet Storrie, with illustrations by Sue Hitchmough (Storrie 1990).

Statues, sculptures, paintings and other art forms of local significance can be found in town squares, marketplaces, municipal gardens and regional museums and galleries all over the country, and indeed this is the case all over the world. Places such as council offices, town halls, fire stations, universities and hospitals are also worth researching to see if they hold important local treasures that give insight into local history.

Sourcing good-quality reproductions of local artwork for the purposes of teaching and learning can be a challenge, however, particularly for less well-known pieces, such as *The Leam near Willes Road Bridge, Warwickshire*. Taking your own digital photographs is usually the answer, but this may not be possible if works of art are displayed in difficult places to access. Also, the quality of a photograph taken with a basic handheld camera will probably not be high enough to magnify a clear image on to an interactive whiteboard or for using with a digital projector.

One charity that is committed to making high-quality images of publicly owned works of art freely available on a digital database is the Public Catalogue Foundation. In partnership with the BBC and 3,000 public collections in the UK, the foundation has already digitized all publicly owned oil paintings[2] in the country and has plans to expand this to other painting media and visual art forms, starting with sculpture, if funding is secured. The oil painting database can be found on the BBC website under the project title Your Paintings.[3]

Amazingly, there are around 200,000 publicly owned oil paintings in the UK, and, even more staggering, 80 per cent of them are in store. Before the Public Catalogue Foundation started to complete an inventory of this geographically fragmented collection, cared for by town and city councils, local authorities and various trusts, knowing about the existence of many of *your* paintings was extremely difficult, and obtaining high-quality reproductions of them was near impossible. The paintings may have been being saved for the nation, but in many cases there was little or no knowledge of this by the general public.

Fred Hohler, the Founder and Chairman of the Public Catalogue Foundation, and former diplomat and financier, became aware of the problem concerning our national asset when he was touring the country tracking down public art for his own pleasure. He was impressed by 'the sheer range, depth and quality of this collection'[4] but astonished at not being able to buy a catalogue when he visited the museum shop at Fitzwilliam Museum in Cambridge. He immediately asked to speak to the curator, who explained that due to a combination of a lack of resources and space, this was a nationwide issue. Fred Hohler endeavoured to do something about it by setting up the foundation, which first published not-for-profit printed catalogues region by region, and then, together with the BBC, placed the digitized images of the paintings online, free of charge, consolidating all the individual parts of the collection as a whole.

As well as being a central deposit for cataloguing the works of art, the Your Paintings website helps to publicize the importance of many of the pieces for illustrating local, national and international history. It does this by asking the public to share their local knowledge about what is depicted in the paintings through the Tagging and Art Detective features. Although not specifically designed as a resource for schools, these offer excellent opportunities for pupils to collaborate in a real-life nationwide digital communication project.

Literacy skills can be developed through the Tagging tool, together with building an understanding of the principles of organizing digital information. Users are prompted to type in words that they think describe what they can see in paintings. Their contribution is added to the list of key words set against the work of art. This helps people searching the database. For example, if a user searches for all the paintings with a particular person in, or landmark, then these will appear in a drop-down list if they have been tagged with the key word. The activity can be undertaken as a whole class on an interactive whiteboard, or on laptops or iPads by small groups or individual students.

Appearing beside every painting, the Art Detective feature asks 'Tell us what you know'. This is a platform for anyone to type in larger amounts of information. It is then sent to the institution holding the painting and, if deemed to be accurate, published online. The intention is that over time, the website will gradually be populated with noteworthy comments from the general public. Some of these could be sent in by school pupils who have undertaken enquiries into local historical figures with portraits on the Your Paintings website, or information that pupils have gleaned about a local place or event portrayed in a painting. Another useful feature, called My Paintings, allows users to curate their own virtual exhibitions in the form of slideshows. They can present these to other users if they wish by adding email addresses.

One of the first educational projects to benefit from the Public Catalogue Foundation digitally photographing the national collection of paintings was Picture This!, an initiative run by Rotherham Metropolitan Borough Council School Effectiveness Service. Since 2007, Picture This! has been challenging schools in Rotherham to use selected pieces of artwork to stimulate cross-curricular teaching and learning. Its aim is to strengthen the quality of learning experiences for pupils outside of core subjects by improving teachers' subject knowledge and confidence in delivering a richer curriculum for children, and by improving pupils' opportunities to visit museums and galleries.

Having previously joined in with the National Gallery's Take One Picture project as a head teacher at two primary schools, Del Rew, a consultant head teacher from the Rotherham Metropolitan Borough Council School Effectiveness Service, who is passionate about the arts in education, introduced the idea to some of the head teachers in Rotherham, including Maggie Duroe, Head Teacher of Wentworth CE Junior and Infant School, an Ofsted 'outstanding' school (2007 and 2009), praised for its exciting curriculum where pupils make rapid progress to reach high standards.

In April 2012, Del described in conversation with me, when we were discussing the origins of Picture This!, how he had gone to the National Gallery as a schoolboy and how it had had a major impact on him. 'I would never have gone unless I went with my school . . . We [the Rotherham Metropolitan Borough Council School Effectiveness Service] were worried that the curriculum in schools was becoming narrower and we wanted to do something about it.'

Wentworth School sent a submission of pupils' work to the 2007 Take One Picture scheme and were exhibited in London. Following this, Maggie Duroe and Sandra Sanders, an arts specialist with Advanced Skills Teacher status at Wentworth CE Junior and Infant School, made a presentation at a conference to Rotherham teachers about their experiences. At the same time, Kevin Madeley, also a former head teacher from the borough working in the effectiveness service, was leading a Book Awards programme in Rotherham with the view to raising achievement and generally enhancing pupils' engagement with their learning. Many of the teachers that he spoke to had seen Maggie and Sandra's presentation and expressed an interest in using the visual arts to teach subjects other than Art and Design. They were also excited about the prospect of celebrating pupil outcomes at a large event locally. From these sparks of enthusiasm, Picture This! was launched, growing every year with more schools joining in with the project: 25 primary schools taking part in 2007/2008, 27 in 2008/2009, 33 in 2009/2010, 54 in 2010/2011, and two special schools and five secondary schools also participating in 2011/2012.

In 2009, the project's steering group[5] chose two focus pictures from the store at Clifton Park Museum, situated in the town, for the annual challenge. One painting, entitled *The Oxley Children* (c.1825) by an unknown artist, was selected because of its local connections. Although the identification of the sitters is not certain, the children in the painting, wearing fashions and playing with games from their own time, are very probably from a family whose fortune was made during the Industrial Revolution from steel production in Rotherham. The other picture, *Asleep on the Watch* (1872) by John Thomas Peele, shows a contrasting nineteenth-century image of a young girl and a baby living in poverty, and although painted in a way that was palatable for Victorian philanthropists, it clearly highlights the struggle of the young girl who has fallen asleep leaning against a baby's cot while peeling potatoes. Is she the baby's sister or mother? If she is the sister, then where are their parents? Are there any clues? Why is there a caged bird in the picture? What can be seen out of the high window? These are all questions that pupils at Rotherham schools posed when exploring the painting.

The paintings were taken out of storage and displayed at Clifton Park Museum for schools to visit over the six-month duration of the project. Luckily, the Public Catalogue Foundation had only recently digitally photographed them (to a very high resolution), so it was possible to supply teachers with high-quality printed and virtual reproductions for using with their pupils back in the classroom. If this had not been the case, the project would have been seriously hindered. The quality and size of a stimulus resource directly impacts on the level of engagement pupils and teachers have with it, and ultimately the standard of the learning outcomes. Neither Clifton Park Museum nor Rotherham Metropolitan Borough Council School Effectiveness Service had the specialist equipment or expertise needed to make high-quality reproductions. Undoubtedly, an inferior reproduction would have reduced the number of schools wanting to get involved.

All 33 schools who took part in the 2009 challenge exhibited their work at a special event at the Magna Centre, an arts and science venue in Rotherham, formerly a steel works site. The appropriateness of the exhibition space, linking so well to the history of the *The Oxley Children* painting, added an extra importance and relevance to the occasion, which opened with a private view for all the pupils, their parents and siblings and, of course, their teachers. Governors and local dignitaries were also invited.

The excitement generated by so many schools simultaneously focusing on the same works of art was infectious and bought about an extraordinary range of cross-curricular work, from Victorian tile designs to models of period interiors and investigations into the history of local industry. The exhibition was so good that it was redisplayed in the town's central Art Gallery during the first month of the school summer holidays, where they recorded double the number of visitors that they would normally expect at that time of the year.

Local appetite to celebrate pupils' achievements from Picture This! continues. A parent governor of one of the schools involved in the project, who owns a printing business in Rotherham, had the idea in 2011, together with a number of other entrepreneurs, of reproducing artwork on a massive scale to display in an open-air exhibition within the town centre, to make it more attractive to visitors and hopefully boost the local economy. Known as Gallery Town,[6] this initiative is backed by Rotherham Local Strategic Partnership Board. Alongside reproductions from Picture This! is artwork from local artists and large-scale prints of famous works of art. Nick Cragg, a local businessman and supporter of Gallery Town said in a press release[7] marking the unveiling of a new series of Picture This! work themed around the Olympics:

> It was always the plan to include artwork by local school children from around Rotherham . . . not just because their work is fantastic, but it also means that each pupil will want to come into the town centre and show off their work to parents, grandparents, cousins, aunties, and uncles.

Picture This! and Gallery Town are both hugely successful projects with a growing following of devotees. They have improved the lives of the people who live in Rotherham by acting as catalysts for change. In transforming the way that schools and the communities in which they belong communicate and work with each other, as a group they have positively enhanced community cohesion and the local economy.

Picture This! has created a culture of collaboration consistent with important findings identified in the 2010 McKinsey Report, *How the World's Most Improved School Systems Keep Getting Better* (Mourshed *et al.* 2010). Analysing the 25 top best-performing school systems in the world, in a follow-up to the 2007 McKinsey report on education (Barber and Mourshed 2007), *How the World's Best-performing Schools Come out on Top*, it found that those on a journey from 'good to great' and 'great to excellent' 'establish collaborative practices between teachers within and across schools that emphasize making practice public . . . that serve to perpetuate and further develop the established pedagogy' (Mourshed *et al.* 2010: 4).

Sadly, opportunities to 'make practice public' between schools in this way are becoming less common due to government budgetary decisions made since the global financial crash. It was observed in Ofsted's 2012 *Making a Mark: Art, Craft and Design 2008–11* that the drastic cutting of advisory services in many local authorities has left teachers more isolated:

> Innovation and leadership of national initiatives at regional level by local authority specialists declined dramatically during this survey. Subject leaders were often too isolated to share best practice between primary, secondary schools and colleges.
> (Ofsted 2012a: 7)

It is important to note here that Picture This! has only survived due to the immense effort and belief of the members of the steering group. It is also a testament to the power of the visual arts that a project such as Gallery Town sees works of art as one solution to an economic crisis.

Notes

1   The East Midlands Museum Buddies website showing examples from a Take One Picture regional project run by Nottingham City Museums and Galleries at: www.mubu.org.uk/takeonepicture/.

2   The Your Paintings database is a photographic catalogue of all the oil, acrylic and egg tempera paintings in UK public ownership (including mixed media artwork with oil, acrylic or egg tempera in them).

3   The Your Paintings database is available on the BBC website at: www.bbc.co.uk/arts/yourpaintings/.

4   Quote from the Foreword by Fred Hohler in the Public Foundation Catalogue, The Fitzwilliam Museum, Cambridgeshire, published in 2006.

5   The Picture This! steering group is chaired by Del Rew (a consultant head teacher from the Rotherham Metropolitan Borough Council School Effectiveness Service), and includes Maggie Duroe (Head Teacher of Wentworth CE Junior and Infant School, Rotherham), Sandra Sanders (an arts specialist with Advanced Skills Teacher status at Wentworth CE Junior and Infant School, Rotherham), Kevin Madeley (a former head teacher from Rotherham and member of the Rotherham Metropolitan Borough Council School Effectiveness Service), Anne Jones (a current head teacher of a Rotherham primary school) and Debbie Hepplestone (a Rotherham secondary Art Teacher).

6   More information about the Gallery Town project is available at: www.gallerytown.org.uk/home/.

7   Gallery Town press release, 15 November 2012.

Part III

Getting a project started

This section aims to support teachers in designing their own cross-curricular projects using the visual arts as a central stimulus. It discusses in detail considerations from the initial planning stage through to implementation, including selecting a work of art, resourcing, strategies for engaging interest among staff, pupils and parents, and ideas around assessment and ensuring progression of learning.

The chapters follow a three-step process – finding inspiration, inspiring others, and celebrating pupils' work. However, it is extremely important to emphasize that creativity is not linear. To get the best results from any creative process, you need to consider it in the round, as well as breaking it up into manageable parts. You need to move backwards and forwards between steps, modifying your ideas as you go. This will maximize its chances of being successful, and with an education project this means maximizing learning opportunities that stretch and challenge all pupils.

Step 1 (Chapter 6): Finding inspiration

This chapter looks at finding your own inspiration for a cross-curricular visual arts project. It identifies the essential knowledge and skills that can be taught through the visual arts and discusses making links with other subject areas.

Step 2 (Chapter 7): Inspiring others

This chapter concentrates on ways to inspire other teachers in a school and how to best engage pupils in a cross-subject visual arts project. First, there are ideas for how to go about developing a shared vision for the visual arts in a school and thoughts on putting those discussions into practice. Second, it looks at shaping short-term and medium-term planning around the needs, interests and prior knowledge of pupils, helping them to make progress across the curriculum.

Step 3 (Chapter 8): Celebrating pupils' work

This chapter focuses on making visible the process of how a project develops, and how this can add value. It discusses the benefits of sharing learning outcomes at the end of a project in a variety of ways, and looks at online opportunities that can lead to improving pedagogy.

Chapter 6

Finding inspiration for a cross-curricular visual arts project

The first thing that you need to do when thinking about starting a cross-curricular project based around the visual arts is to be inspired by a starting point yourself. This can happen in a number of ways. You might be excited by an innovative initiative run by an organization (for example, a scheme run by a museum or gallery or another charity promoting the arts in schools). Alternatively, an encounter with an object, person, or passage from a book or television programme in the course of your everyday life may set off a creative spark that could be developed into an engaging project for pupils at some point.

It is a very good idea to gather your creative sparks together somewhere. There are various ways of doing this, but essentially you want a place where you can collect interesting things that appeal to you and where you can also write down your thoughts. A sketchbook is perfect for this, as it is portable, making it easy to add new things, so that items do not get lost and ideas forgotten. An A4 size one is compact enough to carry in a bag, yet large enough to give you ample room to expand on ideas, reflect, and add related items that you might find later. A good tip is to leave spare pages between entries so that by the time the sketchbook is complete, themes have organically emerged.

Keeping a sketchbook

A sketchbook is a research tool. They can be described as visual diaries or creative journals, although strict chronology is of little importance. What makes these visual records interesting, and useful for planning teaching and learning activities, is the richness of ideas and the links between ideas that they contain.

In my sketchbook, I make my thoughts concrete by recording them in the form of quick drawings, sometimes with labels, and writing down my personal responses to experiences, such as encountering noteworthy works of art – whether seen in art galleries or museums, in books or magazines, on a television programme or on the Internet. I always make sure that I include the location of where I found a work of art, in case I want to return to it at a later date, physically or on a website. I paste in images from leaflets, newspaper cuttings, postcards and printouts. I tape in scraps of materials, such as patterned fabric or textured paper, and write down suppliers' details and the contact names of people who might be able to help with a particular project.

I take my sketchbook on holiday and on day trips with me and write words that come into my mind to describe my experiences: I might be on a beach on a blustery day, or on a wintry walk in a forest, or maybe climbing up the Eiffel Tower. Afterwards, I sometimes look for how other artists have encapsulated similar experiences and add these to my sketchbook. I do not limit this to visual artists, but look at the work of poets, playwrights, lyricists, musicians, dancers or choreographers too. All these ideas, my own work and the work of others can be used to fuel cross-curricular teaching and learning projects.

You may feel that your drawing skills are not good enough to keep a sketchbook, but, as you can see, there are plenty of other ways to record your experiences without having to pick up a pencil; although I would urge you to have a go at drawing, even if it is something that you have not enjoyed doing in the past. The key is to look, look and look again at what you are drawing. There are some drawing activities in the next chapter that you might want to try out. Teachers need to investigate their own creative potential in order to encourage and facilitate pupils to explore theirs.

As well as making sketches, writing words, collecting ephemera and comparing my experiences with other artists' work on the same theme, I take digital photographs, and lots of them. I upload them to a special file on my computer so that I can use them as resources in the classroom at a later date, and I select and print out some to add to my sketchbook. A small camera is ideal for this kind of research. An iPhone, for example, takes perfectly good quality images and is always to hand, being stuffed, as it usually is, in the side pocket of my bag. I like not having to worry about ruining expensive camera equipment.

When taking photographs for research purposes, it is a good idea to:

- **Contextualize things** by including the setting. This will also remind you when and where you saw the work of art. Also, having a person or recognizable object such as a tree stand next to an object will give a sense of scale.
- **Follow each photograph of an object by taking another photograph of any information about it** (such as an exhibition label). This is much quicker than writing down detailed information, and it will be obvious when uploading the images which work of art it refers to.
- **Take a few close-up shots.** The resolution of a photograph of the whole object may not be large enough to see fine detail, especially if used on an interactive whiteboard.
- **Always check if photography is permitted.** Many museums and galleries do allow photographs to be taken as long as a flash is not used, as this can damage exhibits. Some museums and galleries strictly prohibit photography, especially for temporary displays.

If the physical things that you have collected are too large to stick into a sketchbook, you can also use a box to store them in. This will become something of a treasure trove to inspire your planning. However, to avoid it turning into a junk box, try to label the items with information about what motivated you to keep them and where and when they were found or bought. Another good idea is to photograph the object and either file this image on a computer, or print it out and add it to your sketchbook. This will mean that these items can be linked more easily to other ideas that you have documented and help your emerging themes grow.

Some people find multiplatform apps that can be used with smartphones and iPads, such as Evernote[1] and Springpad,[2] useful for capturing and collating their ideas and the things that they see. Notes from these apps can be shared with colleagues via email and Facebook.

Because producing a sketchbook (and perhaps also a treasure box) is an ongoing process, it is perfectly possible to have several 'on the go' at any one time. There are no rules, although you should strive to keep the sketchbook as personal as possible – a space for reflection – rather than undertaking the exercise purely for the purpose of building teaching resources. It will probably be the case that much of what you put in your sketchbook will not be used in the classroom, and this should be viewed as a positive thing. It will mean that you are interacting with the world of the visual arts at your own adult level in things that interest you. The inspiration that draws you to a stimulus needs to be imparted with passion to your pupils, and to do that, you need to fully explore and enjoy the stimulus yourself. The nurturing of personal interests is one reason why teachers find the visual arts such a valuable and stimulating subject area to concentrate upon with their colleagues and with their pupils, and on their own.

Places to be inspired

Creative inspiration can come from anywhere at any time. A holiday might inspire us to cook something new at home, a conversation with someone might trigger off an idea or perhaps reading a newspaper article might galvanize us to take up a hobby.

An obvious place to go to be inspired is a museum or a gallery. Being in a space that is dedicated to celebrating the value of artistic creations fills me with complete joy. We are fantastically fortunate in the UK to have some of the best collections of art in the world, from publicly owned collections that are displayed in nationally funded institutions, such as the National Gallery, the National Portrait Gallery, the Victoria and Albert Museum, the British Museum, Tate Modern, Tate Britain, Tate St Ives and Tate Liverpool, to collections that are housed around the country by charities such as English Heritage and the National Trust. There are also hundreds of other regional museums and galleries of all sizes, some of which are funded by charitable donations, or part publicly financed or privately owned, and many university collections are open to the public (for example, at the Fitzwilliam Museum in Cambridge and the Ashmolean Museum of Art and Archaeology in Oxford).

Artwork can be seen in outside public spaces as well. Monuments and statues commemorate people or events from our past and recent history and pieces are commissioned to create a cultural focus in a city or town centre or large open area, such as a park. Public art of this kind tends to be large and is often controversial because it is difficult to ignore. *The Angel of the North* (1998) by Antony Gormley in Gateshead was famously slated in the newspapers for being an eyesore and costing £1 million of National Lottery money when it was erected in 1998. Now it is treated more as a landmark for the region, contributing to tourism. More recently, on the harbourside at Ilfracombe in north Devon, a 20-metre-high statue of a naked heavily pregnant woman looking out to sea, with her internal organs exposed, divided opinion. Responses to Damien Hirst's *Verity* (2012) from local people, reported in *The Guardian* newspaper on 17 October, ranged from 'Impressive . . . She's a magnet. She's got personality that draws you in' to 'Grotesque . . . it's not my cup of tea, I prefer my art a bit more conventional.' These newspaper clippings would help generate fascinating debates with a class, looking at personal aesthetic taste and public responsibility.

Because art is about grappling with the big questions that we as human beings have to deal with (such as birth, death, love and beauty), expressed by individuals communicating in a language that we as the viewer are in part helping to construct, a small amount of information (or essential knowledge) is useful to fully appreciate what a piece has to offer. Knowing what it is made out of, and perhaps having a go at using the media yourself, really connects the viewer to a piece, as does having an understanding about some of the common ideas and themes that art represents. It is not necessarily important to find a work of art aesthetically appealing to find it interesting.

Establishing essential subject knowledge for the visual arts

What constitutes the essential things one needs to know about the visual arts is subjective. There is no one true list of 'essential knowledge' because any attempt to compose one would inevitably leave important aspects out. One problem is: which artwork does one choose to exemplify a particular art form, media, technique or idea? Because in many cases there is the whole of Art History to choose from, which includes artwork from every culture around the world, past and present, selecting only a few is always going to be a personal choice.

There are some works of art that come to the fore because they were the first major, well-known pieces to experiment in a particular way and were extremely influential because of it. However, one needs to question how these pieces have become so well known and if there are other equally impressive examples that have had less attention given to them. Where Art History legitimizes a canon of the most prominent works of art of all time – those 'usual suspects' that we tend to see printed repeatedly in art books – it also perpetuates a false perception. This is not to say that works of art that many of us believe to be masterpieces are not; I am simply suggesting that we should be open-minded and look at how artists have resolved aesthetic problems cross-culturally and across periods.

With that in mind, here I briefly introduce some basic information that forms the basis of a good starting place for those who want to find out more about the visual arts. Where I do use examples of artists' work to illustrate a point, I do it with the understanding that there are numerous other examples I could have cited, and part of the excitement of learning about the visual arts is to track these down yourself in museums and galleries, in books and on the Internet.

Symbolic references

A fundamental concept to understand about all works of art is that they are representations of the real world. This can be in either a realistic or abstract (distorted) way. René Magritte illustrated this concept brilliantly in his painting *La Trahison de Images* (*Ceci n'est pas une pipe*) (1929), translated from French as *The Treachery of Images* (*This is Not a Pipe*). What he painted was a picture of a pipe and not the pipe itself. Even though he was very straightforwardly painting a pipe, it was still a transcription of something from the real world into another form, in his case a three-dimensional real pipe into a two-dimensional painting of a pipe. The symbolic reference in the painting was the pipe, because the viewer understands the picture of the pipe to represent a real pipe.

Other symbolic references in works of art are more complicated for the viewer to decipher, either because they are abstract, and therefore may not be understood by the viewer as anything that they recognize from the real world, or because the symbol is in itself a representation of something else. This is when the viewer needs to look for clues in the artwork to try to construct a meaning.

References can be culturally linked and belong to a set of codes that are understood only to some people. Cracking these codes, like detectives, is good fun. Try tracing the same object in different works of art, thinking about the contexts in which the artists have placed them. Books explaining signs and symbols can help here, but usually the small amount of information supplied by a museum or gallery, or in an art book, will be all you need. Finding out, for instance, that the Roman goddess Venus is usually shown holding an apple can open up a whole world of storytelling. Characters from all sorts of commonly told stories regularly have attributes (as these objects are known) that can be identified. Symbolic visual language extends to bodily gestures and facial expressions too. These have been formalized in specialist books for artists in the past, but these tend not to be necessary for interpreting artwork because, as in the theatre, the actors in a work of art exude their tale dramatically for the audience.

Any interpretation will ultimately be unique to the viewer as they use their own knowledge and experiences to do this. For example, an image of a realistic landscape may seem to clearly represent a warm summer day in the countryside, but to one viewer it may remind him or her of a favourite childhood walk and memories might come flooding back. Or someone could feel a particular empathy with a sculpture of a male nude weighed down by the whole world on his shoulders, which for others may simply symbolize the Greek god Atlas.

'Reading' symbolic references is part of a person's visual literacy, and is something that we build knowledge of in our everyday lives, interacting with visual culture in the media, and through advertising and with our engagement with different visual art forms. The more exposure we have to art from a variety of periods in time and cultures, the more critically attuned we become to the subtleties of those cultures and the more rewarding our looking experience becomes.

Visual art forms

The term 'visual art form' is used to define different types of visual art. It includes drawing, printmaking, painting, sculpture, photography, and the decorative arts and crafts (for example, textiles, fashion design, interior design, ceramics, metalwork, glassmaking, papermaking and woodwork). Below, I describe the main features of each. There is some overlap with media and techniques. In the first instance of using specialist vocabulary, I have highlighted these in bold. Pupils should be made aware of these terms, and therefore they should be included within your short-term planning under a heading 'key subject-specific vocabulary'.

Drawing

Drawing is a fundamental skill for all artists and is one of the first things that they learn. It is the starting point for most works of art and, in some cases, the final piece as well. Most artists practise drawing regularly. Drawing from life is a discipline that helps improve

first-hand observational skills. This is when artists draw what is in front of them (for example, a person (called a **model**) or a landscape or man-made or natural objects). During the fifteenth and sixteenth centuries, in his famous scientific **studies** of animals, plants and the human body, Leonardo da Vinci used drawing to carefully observe and understand the natural world. Some of these show the whole subject, as well as focusing on smaller areas, rather like a microscope. He also annotated these drawings to give additional information.

Sketching is a drawing technique that artists use to quickly visually record what they see. Small, feather-like marks are made to describe what the artist is looking at. By using these lightly drawn marks, the artist can search for the exact line he or she is looking for. Sketching tends to be done in **sketchbooks** or on paper that can be compiled in a **portfolio**. Sketches can be used to inform more finished pieces of work. One method is to make a full-sized drawing on paper of a final piece, basing this on a number of sketches. This design (called a **cartoon**) can then be transferred to a canvas, or other prepared surface, by pricking small holes along the drawn lines and brushing powdered charcoal through it. Cartoons are also used to produce stained glass windows, tapestries and ceramic tile designs.

The word 'cartoon' has changed over the years to mean a comical drawing, or series of drawings that tell a story. Sometimes, these are made into animated films. Mickey Mouse, created by Walt Disney in 1928, is one of the most famous cartoon characters from the last century, along with action heroes such as Superman. These drawings can tell us many things about the culture of a country at the time they were made. An interesting project for primary-aged children is to compare the cartoons they like with the ones children watch in other countries.

Traditionally, drawings are made using pencils. One benefit is that pencil can be rubbed out if a mistake is made. However, if sketching lines are made lightly, and drawn over when the line that the artist is looking for is found, an eraser should not be necessary. Seeing these exploratory marks gives a drawing a sense of **form** (three-dimensional shape), **movement** and **texture**, and rubbing out can damage the surface that the artist is drawing on, and the mark can often still be seen.

Pencils are graded according to how hard or soft they are. The softer the pencil, the darker the mark it will make. Having a variety of grades to use when drawing enables greater experimentation with **tone** (making light and dark marks). The most useful grades of pencils for sketching purposes are HB (medium grade), 2B (softer) and 4B (softer still).

Artists experiment with drawing in a variety of media, as well as in pencil. You can draw and sketch with marker pens, biros, paint, sticks dipped into ink, wire, literally anything. Prehistoric drawings of animals have been found in caves made from charcoal (burnt wood), chalk and natural pigments, while thousands of years later, graffiti artists are still drawing on walls, now with spray paint.

Printmaking

Drawings can be delicate, so one way that artists try to ensure that these survive over time is to print them. There are different methods of printing. Some methods only produce one image, such as basic **monoprinting**. Here, a drawing is made in ink or paint on a water-resistant surface and then reproduced by evenly pressing paper down on top of it. Multiple copies can be made from other methods, such as **etching** or **lithograph**. With these, a drawing is made on metal **plates** or stone tablets. The plate or tablet is treated with chemicals that wear away the areas where the artist has drawn. This plate is then inked up to make the final prints.

Printing **repeated patterns** or images on paper or fabric can be achieved with carving designs into wooden blocks. This ancient method, called **woodblock printing** (or woodcut printing), can also be done using lino or polystyrene tiles (known as press printing). After the design is cut into the wood or lino, or indented into the tile, a roller is needed to evenly apply the ink. It is then turned over and lined up (**registered**) with the previously printed **motif** (pattern detail or image) and a clean roller is firmly rolled over the back. **Stencils** are also an effective way to print repeated patterns or single motifs that you want to reproduce more than once. For complex designs with more than one colour, a stencil for each colour can be adhered on to a **screen** made of woven mesh, or transferred to a screen using a photosensitive chemical (the photo emulsion technique).

Painting

The subject of a painting (and therefore its purpose) can roughly be classified into different **genres**. (Some of these genres also apply to other art forms.) They are:

- **History painting:** Narrative paintings about real historical events or that tell mythological or religious stories. These are usually on a large scale. They include religious altarpieces and works commissioned for grand houses and castles.
- **Portrait painting:** Paintings that contain information about a real person or a group of people (animals as the sole focus of a painting can be defined as portraiture, although they are sometimes classified as a separate genre). Portraits of powerful people from the past tell us much about the life and times of that person and the country where he or she lived. Fantastic examples of these are held in the National Portrait Gallery, London, including a fine collection of Tudor and Elizabethan portraits, and many modern royal portraits. Before the advent of photography in 1827, portrait paintings were particularly fashionable among affluent families, giving us visual insight into their world. However, we need to be mindful that this is only a partial picture of history, as very few portraits were made of poorer people, unless they were in subservient roles.
- **Landscape painting (also includes seascape, cityscape and townscape):** These are paintings that show a place. This genre became increasingly popular in the nineteenth century through the work of the Romantic artists, in particular J.M.W. Turner and John Constable. Before then, landscape was rarely seen as a suitable subject in its own right and tended to be either part of a history painting (as seen in the work of Claude Lorrain) or part of a portrait composition (for example, those by Thomas Gainsborough). Twentieth-century British examples include the work of Paul Nash and Ben Nicholson.
- **Genre painting:** These paintings show scenes from everyday life, either people working or during times of recreation. These were very popular in the Netherlands in the seventeenth century. Johannes Vermeer is probably the most well-known Dutch genre painter.

- **Still life:** Paintings that show an inanimate object or group of objects. The artist's skill can be shown in how he or she describes in paint the different materials, forms, patterns and textures. Examples include the work of Cézanne, Picasso, Juan Sanchez Cotán, Frida Kahlo and Patrick Caulfield. Still life paintings in which the objects symbolically relate to the theme of life and death are called **vanitas** still life paintings, such as Harmen Steenwyck's *An Allegory of the Vanities of Human Life* (*c.*1640), where musical instruments represent human achievement and a skull and snuffed out lamp represents mortality.

Types of paint

All paint is made from **pigment** (natural or chemical colour) mixed with a binder of some kind to make it stick. The type of paint artists use is dependant on what was available to them at the time they lived and also on what **finish** (look) they want the artwork to have. Being able to experience the feel and smell of high-quality paint enhances the appreciation that one has when looking at a piece that is made in the same materials. For instance, if you see an egg tempera painting (a type of paint used during the Medieval period and Early Renaissance) and have actually had a go at making and using egg tempera yourself, you will empathize more with the artist. You will understand how much time it would have taken to achieve the depth of colour, how quickly the paint dries, making it difficult to **blend** colours, and how the most effective technique is to use **cross-hatching** brushstrokes, one over another to form a cross, and so on. This level of understanding only comes about through first-hand experimentation. However, some paints (particularly oil, acrylic and gouache) are costly, and because budget is an important factor to consider when resourcing a school project, I have included in the list of types of paint below alternative cheaper versions of some paint with similar properties:

- **Egg tempera** (also known as tempera) is made from natural colour pigment (such as lapis lazuli, a semi-precious stone, for blue) mixed with egg yolk. It is quick-drying and was largely superseded by oil paint after 1500. A famous egg tempera **mural** is Leonardo da Vinci's *The Last Supper* (1495–8), painted in the refectory of the Convent of Santa Maria delle Grazie, Milan.
- **Oil paint** is a slow-drying paint made from pigment(s) suspended in drying oil, usually linseed oil. It has a distinctive strong smell. It is not water-soluble, so therefore does not wash out of clothes. A solvent, such as turpentine or white spirit, is needed to clean brushes and can also be used to thin the paint. Before the invention of the metallic collapsible tube (by John Rand in 1841), artists had to mix oil paint as they needed it because it had a short 'shelf life'. Squeezable metal tubes meant that paint was more portable and gave artists greater freedom to paint outside. This was taken full advantage of by the Impressionists. The raised textured effect that is possible to achieve with oil paint is called **impasto**.
- **Acrylic** paint is a modern alternative to oil paint. It is faster-drying and water-soluble. Sold in tubes, the colour pigment is suspended in polymer, a rubber-based solution.
- **Gouache** paint is used to give a flat, matt, opaque finish (no brushstrokes are visible). Book illustrators and graphic designers favour using this paint. Also sold in tubes, the colour pigment has been mixed with gum arabic. It is water-soluble.

Recipe for making egg tempera

You will need: an egg, a brush, water, colour pigment(s) (powder paint or natural pigment(s)).

1   Separate the yolk from the egg white and discard *all* the white (the most effective method is to place the yolk in the palm of the hand, letting the white run through the fingers).
2   Mix the yolk with either a little water and colour pigment(s), or for an emulsion (large coverage) mix, one part water to one part yolk in a sealed jar, and shake vigorously.
3   Paint on to a prepared dry hard surface – traditionally gesso (plaster) on wood or a wall, but a good substitute primer is matt white paint on thick card or wood.

- **Readimix** is a budget paint sold in bottles with similar properties to gouache.
- **Watercolour** paint is sold in blocks of colour pigments that can be mixed by the artist with water. Transparent washes of coloured tints can be layered with very effective delicate results. Detail can be picked out with a small brush using less water. Watercolours are easily portable and usually come as a set in a tray with a mixing palette. Watercolour-quality paper is needed that is thick enough to absorb the water until it is dry, otherwise paper tends to warp. Alternatively, paper can be stretched by immersing a sheet in water, placing it on a wooden board and then sealing all the edges with brown paper tape. A top tip from Mark Hazzard, Head Teacher at Windmill Hill School, Swindon, the inspiration behind the Take One Picture scheme, is to give each pupil a watercolour set that they can refill with blocks of colour when each has run out. He says, 'Because it belongs to them, they look after it better',[3] and therefore it is very cost-effective. The box stays with the pupils, and when they leave they keep it as a reminder of their art experiences at school.
- **Powder paint** is an affordable way to buy watercolour paint for the classroom. Scoops of powder can be put into mixing palettes, although this can be messy and wasteful. If funds are available, watercolour blocks are preferable.

Making a colour wheel: basic colour theory

For anyone who wants to learn about the visual arts, knowledge about how colours are mixed to make other colours, and which colours harmonize together or intensify each other, is essential. The best way to understand this basic colour theory is to make a **colour wheel**:

- On a piece of thick paper or card, draw a large circle with another circle inside that is about two-thirds its size, to create a wheel shape.
- Divide the rim into 12 equal parts. These are your colour areas.
- Paint the first area yellow, the fifth area red and the ninth area blue. These are the **primary colours**. These colours cannot be mixed by other colours.

- Using a palette, mix yellow and red paint together to make orange, painting this in the third area on the rim. Orange is a **secondary colour**.
- Mix red and blue paint together on a palette to make purple. Paint this in the seventh area on the wheel. Purple is a secondary colour.
- Mix blue and yellow paint together to make green. Paint this in the eleventh area. Green is a secondary colour.
- Now make the **tertiary colours** by moving clockwise around the wheel, mixing a primary colour with the nearest secondary colour. Paint each new colour into the area between the two colours that you mix together.

Colours are used by artists to create moods. Colours that are next to each other on the colour wheel can blend into each other and harmonize together. **Shades** of blue and green are **cold colours**, while yellow, orange and red shades are **warm colours**. Colours that are opposite each other on the colour wheel intensify each other when they are placed together. These are known as **complementary colours**.

Sculpture

Sculpture is **three-dimensional**. You can move around it and see it from different sides. Children make three-dimensional models from a very early age with bricks, sand, mud and dough. When their fine motors skills are more developed, they love to make sculptures from empty boxes, sticky tape, glue and paint, and **papier mâché** and **modelling clay**, including plasticine, which is ideal for making models for digital animations.

Professional sculptors tend to use materials that are weather-resistant, especially if the artwork is for displaying out of doors. Using a resistant material means that the piece will last for many years. Some artists **carve** in stone. Michelangelo's celebrated *David* (1500–4) stands over five metres high and is carved from one block of **marble**. Bronze is also a favoured material by sculptors. Instead of carving it, artists use clay or modelling wax to make the sculpture from which a mould is made in a process called **lost wax casting**. Other metals can be cast using the same method.

Sometimes, the materials that sculptors use come from the natural environment. This is called **environmental sculpture**. Well-known examples include *Spiral Jetty* (1970) by Robert Smithson, made from 6,650 tonnes of rock in the Great Salt Lake of Utah, and many works by Andy Goldsworthy. Goldsworthy arranges the beautiful colours and forms that he finds in nature to create sculptures that disappear soon after they have been made. Leaves are blown away in the wind, and snow and ice melts. Photographs are taken to record the pieces, but it is the delicate and ephemeral qualities of the sculptures themselves that carry a poignant message about how human beings and nature can live in harmony.

Sculptures can be made out of any materials. Plaited newspaper covered with strips of more newspaper coated in PVA glue is a popular technique with schools because it is a cheap and pupils can make large-scale models that are fairly light in weight, making storage and display easy. For very large works, a wire **armature** might be necessary to plait the paper around. Newspaper-based sculptures can also be covered in Modrock (plaster bandages) or masonry paint to make them more robust and give them a 'sculpted' look. Modelling with other recycled materials is also well liked by schools because, again, it is cheap to resource and can be part of a broader project focusing on environmental issues.

Famously, artists such as Marcel Duchamp and Carl Andre have used found objects to make sculptures. Duchamp put a urinal in an art gallery and entitled it *Fountain* (1917), and Carl Andre lined up firebricks and called it *Equivalent VIII* (1966). This type of sculpture is known as **conceptual art** because it primarily concentrates on an idea, rather than the skill of the artist.

Photography

Since cameras were first invented in 1827, artists have used photography either as a tool to help them produce their art or as a final piece itself. Photographs are brilliant at capturing a moment in time, something fleeting such as a wonderful sunset, or perhaps a portrait of someone that tells us about a particular point in his or her life. The **composition** (the arrangement of the content) of a photograph can be as considered as any other art form or simply a random snapshot.

Before **digital technology**, artists such as Man Ray, Salvador Dalí and Philippe Halsman experimented with the medium of photography to portray an alternative reality, one in which amazing things were possible. This manipulation of images is now made far easier with software packages, such as Photoshop and SketchBook Express. These enable photographs and digital drawings to be layered on top of each other, effects can be added, and even **stop-motion animation** can be achieved with very little training.

After purchasing the equipment, digital technology has made taking photographs cheap and readily available to most people, particularly on multifunctional devices, such as mobile telephones. Some of these are capable of taking moving images as well. They are a great way of documenting, in pictures, personal perspectives on everyday life. What was once the domain of the **photojournalist** is now possible for millions of people around the world, taking eyewitness accounts of events as they happen, that can appear on the Internet and on television news channels in a very short space of time.

The decorative arts and crafts

The artworks in this category have a practical function, as opposed to being made purely for aesthetic and intellectual purposes (as in painting, sculpture and photography – these artworks are collectively known as the visual fine arts). The decorative arts and crafts include, for example, **textiles, fashion design, interior design, ceramics, metalwork, jewellery-making, glassmaking, papermaking, stonemasonry** and **woodwork**. Its materials and techniques define each of these art forms, although some are linked, such as textiles and fashion design (textiles being the designing and making of fabric, and items made out of fabric, while fashion incorporates fabric into the design of items of clothing and accessories). The term **applied arts** refers to the decoration of functional objects, such as cups and furniture, and is interchangeably used with the term 'decorative arts and crafts', although the application of pattern using traditional methods, such as **mosaic**, is more accurately described as an applied art form.

Designing a cross-curricular project

Everything we teach pupils, in whichever subject area and for every age, should be underpinned with educational purpose. This means that it is important to be clear about what we are teaching and why we are teaching it.

The design of your project will depend on a number of factors:

- What is specified in the National Curriculum. (What do you need to cover?)
- The knowledge and skills that you have identified that the pupils you teach need to learn in addition to the National Curriculum. (Which art form or works of art lend themselves most effectively to enabling this?)
- Your own subject knowledge and skills or opportunities for building on subject knowledge and skills. (Is there expertise in the school community that you can use? Is there an opportunity for you to employ the expertise of other people outside of the school, such as a practising artist?)
- Whether the project feeds into a wider project. (Whole year group, whole Key Stage, whole-school, regional project, national project.)

What you teach children should either be part of their statutory entitlement from the National Curriculum or something that you have decided on, either as an individual class teacher or as a team of teachers in a school, which pupils need in addition to this. These needs can either be knowledge- or skills-based. They could address a single pupil's needs, or a particular group of pupils' requirements, the needs of a whole class, or a year group, or a Key Stage or the whole school. It is vital to acknowledge that the National Curriculum only instructs on minimum requirements and that the remainder of the school day should be designed by teachers around the interests and needs of their pupils. These needs should be gauged as part of teachers' ongoing formative assessment and could include, for example, a need for pupils to work more independently, or more collaboratively, or given more opportunities to express their own imaginations.

As well as helping pupils to master technical art skills, the visual arts offer pupils the opportunity to develop skills that are transferable across the curriculum. These are known as key skills. These skills can be improved through the designing and making of artwork, through learning about other people's art and the culture and time that art belongs to, and through using artwork as a stimulus for expressing ideas in other ways. The list below gives examples of how the visual arts aid the development of pupils' literacy, numeracy, research, problem-solving and evaluation, presentation, and personal skills.

Literacy skills

- Forming opinions and talking about their own work and the work of others, including that of professional artists, past and present.
- Writing about their artwork and the work of others, including using artwork as a stimulus for writing imaginatively.
- Responding to artwork as a form of text by interpreting meaning and giving reasons for these ideas.

- Using artwork to find out about other cultures and different languages. For example, naming the items in a work of art using vocabulary from the artist's own language.

Numeracy skills

- Understanding the properties of shapes (2D and 3D), including making models using and creating geometric forms.
- Describing the position and movement of shapes, including reflective symmetry, rotation and repeated patterns.
- Understanding scale and calculate areas (for example, calculating the size of original works of art).

Research skills

- Gathering information from different sources, making judgements about accuracy and reliability.
- Sorting information and selecting the most appropriate for maximum effect.

Problem-solving and evaluation skills

- Hypothesizing about ideas or items in a work of art using the limited information an artist gives the viewer (for example, what an object might look like in the round if only represented two-dimensionally – the back of a dress in a fashion illustration that only shows the front, or how a winding mechanism might work on an object that is described visually in a painting, or what might happen next in a story).
- Understanding a 'brief' – understanding what is being requested and responding to this.
- Following a design process: from initially generating lots of ideas, then evaluating these to select the most appropriate, refining and modifying these, and presenting a final piece.
- Being prepared to think ambitiously, taking creative risks through plenty of experimentation and having confidence in one's own ability.

Presentation skills

- Being able to express oneself clearly, both visually and through written and spoken words.
- Thinking about how to communicate with different audiences within and beyond the school (links to literacy skills).
- Using digital technology to present ideas, including PowerPoint presentations, using apps, blogging, broadcasting online (links to literacy skills).

Personal development skills

- Listening to and understanding other people's ideas and perspectives.
- Showing resilience by working hard, attempting new things and completing an activity from start to finish.

Table 6.1 Examples of cross-curricular themes using the visual arts as a central stimulus.

Theme	Visual art stimulus	Subject areas
Tudors	Tudor portraits by Hans Holbein and others	Art, History, English
The Industrial Revolution	*An Experiment on a Bird in the Air Pump* (1768) by Joseph Wright of Derby; *The Oxley Children* (c.1825) by an unknown artist; *Rain, Steam and Speed – The Great Western Railway* (1844) by J.M.W. Turner	Art, History, Technology, Science
The Victorian era	*Asleep on the Watch* (1872) by John Thomas Peele	Art, History, Citizenship
The human body	*Verity* (2012) by Damien Hirst; *Little Dancer Aged Fourteen* (1880–1, cast c.1922) by Degas; *David* (1500–4) by Michelangelo	Art, Science
Water/awe of nature	*The Great Wave of Kanagawa* (1831) by Hokusai; *Spiral Jetty* (1970) by Robert Smithson	Art, Science, RE

- Thinking independently and being able to collaborate with others.
- Being involved in developing and improving one's own learning and displaying a positive attitude towards one's work and others' work.

When you have decided which visual arts knowledge and skills you want to teach in the project, including which transferable key skills, you need to think about which work, or works, of art would make a suitable stimulus (as long as high-quality reproductions can be sourced) and which other subject areas might be taught under the umbrella of a thematic approach. Cross-curricular links to the visual art stimulus should be natural and make sense to the pupils. They should not be forced. The following ideas are taken from examples of works of art already cited in this book. Obviously, there are many other examples of themes and artwork that you could use. For instance, you could think about choosing a stimulus or theme that is of local significance or something topical.

The next step in designing a cross-curricular project is to detail the specific knowledge and skills you want to teach for each subject area and to draft engaging activities that will offer pupils opportunities to develop these. An efficient way of doing this is with a mind map. Place the stimulus or theme (using words or pictures) in the centre of a large sheet of paper and write subject area headings radiating from it. It is here that you describe what the pupils will be learning and how they will be learning it, drawing out links between subject areas by matching the same or similar knowledge and skills. It is also the place to add information about additional stimuli that will engage pupils, such as how a project might be launched with a trip to a museum or gallery, or by having an artist resident in school, or perhaps booking an artist for a Skype interview. The end goals of the project should celebrate achievements by drawing together learning outcomes, perhaps from different classes of children, in events such as whole-school assemblies that parents are invited to, exhibitions (in school, online, in the local neighbourhood, or as part of a wider arts initiative), or the unveiling of the piece of artwork that will permanently be on display, or the publication of a special book celebrating the pupils' work. As far as possible, also to try to harness the interests and talents that you have, as well as those of your colleagues, the pupils in your class and other members of the school's wider community.

Notes

1 Evernote app is free of charge and available at: http://evernote.com/.
2 Springpad app is free of charge and available at: http://springpad.com/about.
3 From an interview with Mark Hazzard in the *Times Educational Supplement*, 2 June 2006.

Chapter 7

Inspiring others

Getting staff on board

The visual arts can sometimes be perceived in schools as an activity to fill time when other tasks have been completed, or as a way of occupying pupils who have been removed from a class, or as a reward for good behaviour. Sometimes the quality of art activities are so unchallenging, like colouring-in worksheets, that pupils are switched off to Art as a subject altogether. This can perpetuate an attitude that Art is less important than other subjects.

For the purposes of gaining an understanding of how the visual arts are taught in your school, with the ambition of integrating them as meaningfully as possible into the fabric of a curriculum, it is productive to start a dialogue with colleagues on how they perceive the role of the visual arts within education.

A valuable exercise can be to adopt a noticeboard in the staffroom. This will be the visual arts communication hub. Initially, write two questions in very large print on the noticeboard. This will grab people's attention and is a way of gauging different perspectives. The questions could be phrased as:

- What do you think pupils learn from the visual arts?
- Are these outcomes important?

Advertise that there will be a chance to discuss the questions at a forthcoming meeting. Ask for thoughts to be shared on Post-it notes or labels stuck to the noticeboard over the course of a week or more. This will give people a chance to reflect and discuss ideas among themselves in the first instance. You could also ask people to bring along to the meeting examples of any good-quality learning they have seen that has a visual arts focus, particularly if it is cross-curricular. This could be something that they have done with their own class or seen elsewhere.

At the meeting, make it clear that you are exploring how the visual arts are currently being taught in the school, with a view to discussing whether potential benefits are being fully exploited across subject areas. Answers provoked by your two original questions will be good starting points for this debate, as will looking at any learning outcomes from examples brought in as models of good practice. It will be important for the members of staff bringing in these examples to critique what they believe pupils learnt from the visual arts activity and why the outcomes were important.

Take examples along with you to the meeting too. These could include ideas from the case studies in Part II. The Articulate project (see page 24) can be used to explain how the visual arts can be a focus for creative writing. Evidence gathered from the Take One Picture scheme (see page 35) could demonstrate how using a painting as a central stimulus can allow teachers lots of flexibility to personalize learning by offering pupils opportunities to determine the direction of a project. The Take One Picture approach also promotes experiential learning and genuinely nurtures the interests of pupils, staff, parents and other people connected with the school. The Your Paintings online digital database (see page 59, note 3) can be shown as an excellent resource for exploring and sharing artwork of local significance. And finally, the Picture This! project (see page 56) can demonstrate how people in a whole region can be united through the appreciation of the visual arts as a powerful learning medium.

At a point when people have been allowed time to express their ideas, and also their concerns, it would be a good idea to align the benefits of the visual arts with how Ofsted judge 'outstanding' provision, as found in the *Schools Inspection Handbook 2012* (Ofsted 2012b). The overall effectiveness of a school is graded 'outstanding' if the 'thoughtful and wide-ranging promotion of pupils' spiritual, moral, social and cultural development enables them [the pupils] to thrive in a supportive, highly cohesive learning community.' A school needs to have 'a rich and relevant curriculum', where pupils have 'excellent educational experiences' that 'ensure that they are very well equipped for the next stage of their education, training or employment' (Ofsted 2012b: 27). The quality of teaching in a school is graded outstanding if 'teachers use well-judged and often inspirational teaching strategies' where 'the teaching of reading, writing, communication and mathematics is highly effective and cohesively planned and implemented across the curriculum' (Ofsted 2012b: 36). You could emphasize during the meeting that Ofsted's 2012 *Making a Mark: Art, Craft and Design 2008–11* reported that:

> In all phases of education, pupils' and students' spiritual, moral, social and cultural development grew through topics that embraced their personal interests and experiences. They responded powerfully and sensitively to emotive themes when well taught. However, links with related areas of the curriculum were under-developed.
>
> (Ofsted 2012a: 7)

From the conversations you have with staff, you should be able to ascertain if there is a general consensus about how the visual arts are taught in the school, and if there is a shared desire to develop this further across the curriculum. If so, you should start gathering common opinions and propose these as preliminary statements for a shared vision. Statements might start with, 'As a staff, we believe that the visual arts are important because . . .' Words that characterize creative and inclusive pedagogical practice may feature in the statements, such as innovative, dynamic, imaginative and pupils taking more ownership of their learning.

These statements can then be presented on the visual arts noticeboard for everyone to tweak and add comments and ideas to until people are content that all voices have been heard. The shared vision can form part of a more extensive spiritual, moral, social and cultural development policy, and be used to illuminate decision-making around planning more creative opportunities for pupils.

Other questions that will need addressing as a consequence of preparing a shared vision for the visual arts in a school are:

- How do the statements relate to the school's mission statement?
- What visual arts skills are within the school already and where are there gaps in relevant skills? An audit could be done of the relevant qualifications, experiences and interests of staff and the talents of members of the wider community (parents, governors, alumni).
- What local resources could be employed to the greatest advantage? Can partnerships be brokered with local museums and galleries or local creative industries? Are there artists, designers or authors living nearby that would be willing to work with the school?
- As a whole school, are there any weaknesses that we would like to address as part of a visual arts cross-curricular initiative? From my experiences with helping many schools design their curriculum around the needs of their pupils, and the needs of the communities that they belong to, most teachers (primary and secondary) agree that their pupils need more opportunities to develop independent thinking skills, and the confidence-building that is associated with this, and to improve their understanding and knowledge of the world in order to gain respect for their own and other cultures. Both of these key broad learning objectives can be delivered through using the visual arts at the centre of a cross-curricular project, which, at the same time, can also offer opportunities for pupils to learn other statutory requirements outlined in the National Curriculum.

Putting discussions into practice

If feedback from staff to develop the way that the visual arts are taught in the school is enthusiastic, then a plan can be drawn up that will transform the shared vision into practice.

Staff may identify that they need some professional development input with the visual arts, in which case an audit can be undertaken to determine what skills and interests already exist within the school community. Sending a request to staff, governors and parents asking if they have artistic talents that are perfected to a level that they would be willing and able to share with others is a good idea. One school in Nottingham that did this found out that a parent was an architectural model-maker and this formed the basis of an Art and Maths project, where the parent taught a whole class of Year 6 pupils how to make a three-dimensional model of a two-dimensional image. Other schools have discovered that parents have expert carpentry or dressmaking skills, or that a governor has a beautiful collection of watercolour paintings of birds of prey, or that a teacher has a secret passion for pottery! How these talents are harnessed in the school depends on the appropriateness of the skill in connection with planned learning objectives for a project, the level that the skill can be shared at, the availability of specialist equipment, and the ability of the person to impart his or her knowledge to either just staff, or pupils as well.

Another idea can be to enlist an artist in residence. Working with creative practitioners over a sustained period of time can bring fresh perspectives and enable teachers and pupils to learn in new ways. Ofsted's 2012 *Making a Mark: Art, Craft and Design*

2008–11 reported, 'Work with creative practitioners raised pupils' aspirations and achievement in primary and secondary schools, but this was rarely an entitlement' (Ofsted 2012a: 6). The artistic process of searching for inspiration, experimenting with ideas and making something original from these is made visible by having an artist set up his or her studio in a school. In this environment, curiosity and creativity are highly valued, with a research-based methodology being modelled that can be emulated by everyone. In schools following the Reggio approach (as discussed on pages 12–13), the practising artist (the *atelierista*) works very closely alongside the teachers (the *pedagogistas*), who set the educational agenda, where the content of the curriculum is organically formed around the enquires of the preschool children. Clarity in defining roles, and the relationship between these, is one of the reasons why the Reggio approach is so successful. If you are planning to recruit a creative practitioner at your school, establishing the relationship between an artist in residence, and their work, and the role of the teachers, and the needs of the pupils, is crucial from the very outset.

Here is a checklist of things to consider when recruiting an artist in residence:

Budget – What funding do you have available for the whole project? This needs to include the artist's fee and his or her expenses (for example, insurance or transport costs, if these are going to be charged separately); materials for making the artwork (including materials for pupils to experiment with); any costs for other resources, such as large reproductions of images or hiring or buying specialist equipment; costs for visits out of the school (for example, to a gallery or museum); and any costs for celebrating the work (a special event or publication). It may be possible to share the costs of an artist with another nearby school. An option could be for the artist to have a studio in more than one school and to divide his or her time between these. Seeking funding from arts charities is very worthwhile, although time needs to be built into your planning schedule for a proposal to be drawn up, submitted and a decision waited for.

Art form – Which art form are you interested in? Do you have the specialist equipment, do you need the artist to supply this, or do you have funds to hire what is needed?

Where to find an artist – You need to be clear about the difference between people who are professional artists (therefore, they sell their work or are employed for their artistic skills) and people who practise art as a pastime, or who are in training to be professional artists. The amount they charge will reflect their experience, although you may also find that very experienced professional artists like to work with schools free of charge and expect to only have their expenses covered.

Places to contact:

- Your local authority may have a directory of artists with experience of working in schools in your area.
- You could contact schools directly that you know have worked with artists before. Recommendations and references are undoubtedly the most reliable way for ensuring that you make a quality appointment.
- Museums and galleries often employ freelance artists to lead workshops for children. They may be able to pass on the details of someone who they think would be suitable.

- Your local university might run art courses and have students who are keen to gain valuable experience working with children. Ofsted's 2012 *Making a Mark: Art, Craft and Design 2008*–11 reported that 'The role of college students in inspiring pupils and students in schools was underdeveloped' (Ofsted 2012a: 6).

Once you have found an artist that you think you would like to work with, you should invite him or her into school for a formal interview. This will be a chance for you and the head teacher, and other members of staff, to discuss your objectives, to look through the artist's portfolio and to think about potential ideas. You will need to check that the artist has an up-to-date Enhanced Criminal Record Bureau (eCRB) certificate that has been issued by their employer. If they do not have one, then this will need to be done prior to them starting their residency by your local authority.

When discussing your objectives for the residency with the artist, he or she will need to know:

- The reason for the project (you can outline the school's shared vision for the visual arts).
- What his or her role will be in this vision (you will need to explain the creative cross-curricular pedagogical approach and how this needs to involve the pupils in devising projects, as well as defining the responsibilities of the artist, the teachers and the head teacher).
- The terms and conditions of the employment (a contract will need to be drawn up and signed by the head teacher and the artist, stating responsibilities).
- How long will his or her residency last?
- Where will he or she be based? Will this be in a studio space or will he or she be peripatetic, moving between classrooms, or both? Will he or she be working with one school or several?
- How many pupils will he or she be working with during the project? How will this be structured? Workshops with groups of pupils? Drop-in sessions at break times and after school? (For parity of opportunity, all pupils within the same year group should be given the same chance to work with the artist.)
- How will the planning of the projects be undertaken? In a co-participatory way with a designated teacher or group of teachers? Will this include separate professional development sessions for teachers or will the teachers learn alongside the pupils?

As part of the vision at your school, staff may decide that they would like to dedicate timetable space to working in a more cross-curricular way. This could take the shape of regular slots being allocated to cross-curricular themes or organizing specific events, such as art days, an art week or an 'enrichment' event.

Art days and weeks can be great ways to launch a new project. By collapsing the timetable so that a significant stretch of time is spent discovering interesting visual arts stimuli, pupils can learn about the benefits of concentrated exploration and experimentation. However, in general, teachers find that art days and weeks restrict pupils' opportunities for critical reflection about their learning, and that the advantages in allowing pupils to study a subject intensely over a short period can be curtailed by this. For deep learning to take place, and for knowledge and skills to be secured, ideas need to be formulated by pupils and staff in a process that hands over control between the two in a learning environment that recognizes that ideas can take time to mature. These ideas need to be tested out, and therefore scope is needed to continue enquiries relating to the themes provoked by the art days and week after these have taken place.

The most successful way of dedicating time to the visual arts as part of a cross-curricular teaching and learning approach is to design and implement a creative curriculum. This is one that allows pupils to apply the knowledge and skills that they have learnt in meaningful ways that encourage them to express their own ideas. An effective strategy for achieving this goal is to teach some subjects discretely and apply what is taught to a theme that encompasses a number of subject areas. This model of learning also makes it more likely that transferable skills are being taught at the right challenging level for each individual student across the curriculum.

The amount of time allocated to thematic teaching in the timetable can be a whole-school or an individual teacher's decision, although limiting the time spent on project work to only an hour or so a week should be avoided because this is tokenistic and counterproductive, as pupils will be enthusiastic about the project and full of ideas, yet unable to capitalize on these. Some schools teach core subjects discretely in the mornings and other foundation subjects through a thematic approach in the afternoons. With this model, three or four subject areas can be focused on across the duration of a project, with the addition of practising basic literacy and numeracy skills. It is important, however, not to make too many cross-curricular links, because then projects have a tendency to become overcrowded and confusing. It will probably be the case that different year groups at different times in the school calendar spend varying proportions of their week or term learning through a thematic approach. Flexibility in timetabling will bring about the best results.

Different themes can be chosen by individual classes or Key Stages, or a theme can be the focus for a whole school. Many schools decide to have several whole-school focuses a year, with the remaining time in the term being given to class-based themes. There is no doubt that a project that encourages mass participation in a school, especially one that culminates in an event of some description, galvanizes people into action, creating a purposeful and exciting learning environment that everyone can enjoy – pupils, teachers and parents included. However, it is also the case that if pupils are going to be taught knowledge and skills that are shaped around their different needs at specific times in their school careers, then class-based themes are equally appropriate for much of the year.

Of course, all themes do not need to have a work of art as a central focus. Books, plays or music, to name only a few other rich stimuli, can brilliantly engage pupils' imaginations too. But, as I have hopefully so far convinced you, the visual arts work exceptionally well as an anchor for a cross-curricular project, and this is especially true for a whole-school project. This is because a work of art can enable children and adults of all ages and abilities to:

- have their own response and set their own lines of enquiry;
- link different subject areas together, therefore making learning more meaningful and relevant; and

• improve questioning skills, giving opportunities for imaginative and divergent thinking, and reinforcing a pedagogical approach that views asking searching questions as a fundamental skill for deep learning.

Selecting a work of art as a central stimulus

Many themes that are popular in primary schools are popular with artists too, making it relatively easy to find works of art that will enrich a chosen project. Table 6.1 (see page 76) identifies how the portraits of Hans Holbein will illuminate the life and times of the Tudors for pupils in a joint Art, History and English project; how images showing different people's reactions to innovative technology during the Industrial Revolution will aid children's understanding of the era for an Art, History, Technology and Science topic; and how scientific and aesthetic conversations can be initiated by artwork based on The Human Body or looking at The Awe of Nature.

Filling up your sketchbook (or sketchbooks, if you have been busy) with interesting works of art that you have come across in the course of your everyday life, and recording your responses to them, will mean that you have lots of ideas to hand when developing thematic projects. If, for instance, you were thinking of studying The Seasons, you might have images in your sketchbook that you can use as starting points cut out from magazines, or exhibition guides or postcards. The stunning landscapes of the late nineteenth- and early twentieth-century artist Gustav Klimt would work well here, or the personifications of the seasons by David Teniers the Younger from the seventeenth century. You may have photographs of contemporary environmental sculptures (for example, by Andy Goldsworthy or by local artists who have had pieces commissioned for a sculpture park that might be near your school). These could all inspire descriptive writing from pupils or similar artwork looking at contrasting climates to ours, or perhaps even the designing and making of a sculpture trail in the grounds of the school.

A work of art that you see might also spark off an idea for a theme itself. Recently, I saw a huge interactive installation of four sculptures based on the four elements of fire, water, air and earth in the Garden of Surprises at Burghley House, Northamptonshire. These, I thought, would make superbly engaging stimuli for a cross-curricular Art and Science project.

Ideas from your sketchbook can be followed up on the Internet. In the information age in which we live today, having the world of art at our fingertips is truly amazing. Many museums, galleries and archives across the globe now make their collections, or at least highlights from them, available online. You may also find digital services such as Culture 24[1] or The Space[2] useful starting places to search for current cultural events.

Like all information on the Web, the quality is variable. In general, the website of the organization that holds a particular work of art will be the most reliable source about its origins (called provenance). Other facts about the work will also usually be available (for example, its dimensions and the materials it is made out of). All you really need is a small amount of information and high-quality reproductions of the works that you wish to concentrate on. If an artwork is being used for a sustained project, then a physical print should be used alongside any digital image to aid recall when the interactive whiteboard or individual computers are switched off

The holding organization's website should also be the best place to find out where to obtain a good quality printed and/or virtual image of the artwork. In some cases, this will be a virtual image directly downloaded from the website free of charge, but restriction for its use may apply. For high-resolution images, a separate license may need to be sought and copyright fees paid for. Some collections may signpost you to a digital archive that manages their virtual collection on their behalf within a larger database. Two examples of these archives are Bridgeman Art Library,[3] a commercial company that acts on behalf of museums and galleries internationally, and Your Paintings,[4] an online database run by the charity the Public Catalogue Foundation with the BBC and 3,000 UK public collections (a project described in more detail in Chapter 5). Another database that allows people to search online a growing number of museum and gallery collections from around the world is Google Art Project.[5] As well as containing high-quality images of artwork, this innovative website enables the viewer to virtually walk around the museum and gallery spaces, stopping in front of exhibits as they choose. With the enticing strapline 'Famous artwork in ridiculous detail', it is a Web resource that has the potential to wow pupils in the classroom.

Perhaps a downside of being able to access almost everything all of the time online is that it is easy to be guilty of preserving our own tastes at the expense of not keeping abreast with what is new and innovative. This can happen with our taste in music and film, as well as art. For example, instead of just being interested in the music we liked when we were in our late teens and twenties, we should try to find out about what music is popular today, discovering who won the latest Mercury Prize and who is on the Radio 1 playlist. We need to look at what is happening now, and how this connects to the past (recent and long-term) to understand what practices and themes are enduring across time and cultures, and which artists' work are exemplars of these. This underlines again the importance of introducing pupils to a range of artworks from different cultures and times not just from the past, but also from the present. Push yourself, and the teachers you work with, to find out about which artists have looked at similar themes to others across periods. Do some research into current exhibitions in major cities. Actively seek out who has won the latest Turner Prize and who represented Britain in the most recent Venice Biennale. This embracing of the world of art will help you and your colleagues avoid just showing pupils the usual suspects, such as van Gogh's *Sunflowers* (1888), da Vinci's *Mona Lisa* (*c.*1503–6) and Constable's *Hay Wain* (1821). Of course, there is absolutely nothing wrong in introducing these iconic masterpieces to children, and they should be aware of them, but not *only* them.

Here are other things to be mindful of when selecting a work of art as a central stimulus:

- Be open to showing pupils artwork that does not necessarily aesthetically appeal to you. For an artwork to sustain educational interest over the course of a cross-curricular project, it may not be a piece that you would like to hang on your wall at home or put in your garden.
- Effective learning needs to be within the realm of pupils' experiences; therefore, any work of art selected for teaching and learning purposes needs to relate in some way to the lives of the children that you are teaching.

- Young children analyse art from a realist perspective. Art that relies on the comprehension of abstract concepts, such as metaphor, will only be seen by them in terms of shape and colour. With maturity, children gain the ability to imagine things from different points of view, and this is essential for understanding the complexities of much abstract art.
- In my experience, there is far too much emphasis by teachers on artists' biographical information. Facts about an artist's schooling and circumstances of their death tend to be weighted over more important information that helps children to interpret the meaning of the content of the artwork, such as contextualizing it within its cultural setting. This does not seem to be the case in schools with authors or poets, or scientists and mathematicians. We teach children about the celebrated works of Dickens and Shakespeare foremost through the critical analysis of the texts, not the life histories of the individual writers. We do not teach pupils about the biographical facts of Edward Jenner or Pythagoras or Fibonacci before, if at all, we tell them about their amazing discoveries. So, why is it the norm to introduce children to art with information that is not actually about the art that they are looking at? Teachers need to concentrate more on developing children's skills of observation, extending their visual language, and encouraging pupils to make connections between the content of the art, the art of other people, and how these relate to the children's own lives.

Inspiring pupils

Because pupils' needs should drive any curriculum, it is important from the outset of your planning that you think carefully about how a project can be shaped to meet these at an appropriate level of challenge. This means that the educational purpose of a potential project should be identified in the very early stages of development, where National Curriculum objectives and any additional objectives that you have set your particular pupils are clear. You need to ask what knowledge and skills you want pupils to develop (for a cross-curricular project, this will be from a variety of subject areas) and how your planning gives pupils opportunities to develop them.

What are you teaching and why are you teaching it?

- What subject knowledge?
- Which subject-specific skills (such as those involved in making art)?
- Which transferable skills (for example, literacy skills, numeracy skills, research skills, problem-solving skills, presentation skills or personal development skills – see pages 74–5 for more detailed information about transferable skills)?

To ensure progression in pupils' learning, knowledge and skills need to be taught to an increasingly more complex level. American psychologist Jerome Bruner described this as a 'spiral curriculum' in his book *The Process of Education* (1960). The level at which an aspect of a subject is taught depends on the prior knowledge and understanding of the pupils. This means that there will most probably always be children needing to work at different levels in any one class. In your short-term planning, these differences in needs should be reflected in the success criteria for the lesson, or series of lessons, and linked to the learning objective(s):

- Learning objective(s) = What knowledge and/or skills are pupils developing?
- Success criteria = What level (or levels) are they learning them at? What outcomes are you expecting to see?

Crucially, to help pupils improve their learning, they need to be clear about what they are aiming towards, so any feedback needs to be framed around what the next level of expectation might look like. Success criteria help to articulate this to pupils, and should be used to plan next steps for individuals and to shape the learning objectives and activities for subsequent lessons. This may involve, for example, structuring opportunities for mixed-ability group working where those pupils reaching a high level of achievement are grouped with pupils who need to see results at the next level. The Russian psychologist Lev Vygotsky defined this distance 'between the actual development level as determined by independent problem-solving and the level of potential development as determined through problem-solving under adult guidance or in collaboration with more capable peers' as the zone of proximal development (Vygotsky 1978: 89).

The teaching strategies that you use to meet the objectives of the project will vary depending on the needs of the children in the class. To find out their prior knowledge and understanding about a chosen art stimulus, a successful technique is to leave a printed reproduction of the painting, sculpture, piece of textiles, or whatever art form it is, for a week somewhere visible in the classroom, with a question posted next to it, such as 'What do you think of this sculpture?' or 'What would you like to find out about this painting?' Good methods for gathering and sharing pupil responses include a graffiti wall, or asking them to write questions on pieces of card that can be pegged on to a washing line, or to record their thoughts into a Dictaphone. You could also use a mind map format for this exercise, with an image of the artwork in the centre of a piece of paper with plenty of space for pupils to write their questions about what they would like to find out about it around the outside. It could be a huge whole-class mind map, or one shared between a small group of pupils, or one for individuals. Each has its own merits. If pupils are encouraged to add to it throughout the duration of a project, a whole-class mind map can be helpful in tracking what questions and thoughts are provoked over a period of time. A smaller group mind map can show good evidence of shared thinking, where the teacher asks pupils to write down their thoughts and questions after peer-to-peer conversations. The teacher can intervene when appropriate to move learning forward, perhaps posing additional questions starting, 'What if . . .?' An individual mind map is an excellent device for assessing the depth of each pupil's understanding, their willingness and ability to communicate their ideas in writing, and their confidence in following up their ideas. Again, if they are encouraged to return to it over the course of the project, it can show unfolding ideas and can be one way of knowing when pupils are learning what we want them to learn.

Ideas from the mind maps, and other initial questions that come about through introducing the artwork to the children, should inform the design of the overall project. The main objectives need to be set by yourself as the class teacher, or, if working with other teachers, by a team of people, because you are the professionals and you know what the pupils need to learn to enable them to progress further. However, to ensure that you are building on the pupils' prior knowledge, and to maximize pupil engagement, some space needs to be given for pupils to genuinely influence the direction of their work. Take this into account when planning. On the whole, it is best to make a skeleton medium-term plan, including your learning objectives, and to populate this over the course of the project with ideas generated by all those involved. This way, everyone can invest in the learning.

Depending on whether it is necessary to book trips or gather more resources or to liaise with other members of staff, the project can either start straight after the initial questioning exercises, or some time later. Many schools like to introduce the stimulus to the pupils at the end of the preceding half-term (a 'soft' launch) so that staff and pupils can germinate ideas over the holidays.

To make it obvious when the project properly starts (the 'hard' launch), it is important to communicate with the children what they are going to be doing and what they are going to be learning. It needs to be clear how the project fits into their other work and if the project is going to involve other classes or schools, and, if so, how this will happen. Supply them with the following information:

- Which subject areas are part of the project, and which are not?
- How much time are they going to spend on the project? One day? One week? Is it going to take place over a period of a number of weeks? Which days in the week? How many hours a week?
- Are there specific transferable skills that they will be developing during the course of the project (for example, research skills, problem-solving skills, presentation skills or personal development skills)? Are there skills that are going to be taught discretely at other times of the day/week that are also going to be applied to the project, such as specific literacy or numeracy skills?

They will also need to know about any special events that are being organized as part of the project. This might be a visit to a museum or gallery or a trip to the place that is the subject of the artwork, such as a park, a building or an event. Are they going to be working with another member of staff on the project or a visitor to the school, such as a practising artist? Are you joining in with a regional or national project, and what might this entail?

Learning from museums and galleries

Most large museums and galleries offer services for schools. Typically, these consist of some of the following:

- Expert-led guided tours from the staff at the museum or gallery. Some sites offer in-role guides (for example, seeing a collection from the perspective of a Victorian maid). English Heritage provide this service at some of their 400 sites and, in many cases, have replica period clothes that pupils can try on.
- Expert-led themed workshops taken by the staff at the museum or gallery (these can be practical art workshops or object-handling sessions).
- In-house 1:1 training for teachers from expert museum or gallery staff.

- Continuing Professional Development courses for teachers.
- The option for teachers to lead self-guided activities in the museum or gallery.
- Themed worksheets or trails (usually for small groups only).
- Audio trails (handheld or headphone sets that tell the viewer about highlights from the collection, usually for small groups only).
- Themed activity packs (mainly designed as family learning activities, but these can also be engaging for small groups of pupils who are supervised).
- Lunch and cloakroom facilities dedicated to schools.
- Coach parking.
- Outreach services (including loan boxes, visits to schools by museum and gallery staff, competitions and schemes for schools and Skype interviews).
- Online digital resources directed at schools.
- Online digital databases of collections.

After researching what services are available in the museums or galleries (or other sites) that are applicable to the subject of your project, you need to think carefully about what you want the pupils to learn from using them. For instance, do any of the themed services (guided tours, workshops, offers of CPD, trails, activity packs or outreach) support pupils in learning the knowledge and skills that you are intending to focus on? Is there a particular work of art, or works of art, that you want pupils to study? Would an outreach service, such as a loan box or Skype interview with a curator, be the best way of achieving your objectives, or would a visit to the museum or gallery be a more effective way of learning? If so, are there practical matters to address, such as cost, risk assessment, adult-to-pupil ratios, and access to buildings and transport for wheelchair users.

If it were up to me, every child would physically visit a museum or gallery with their class at least once in their school careers, ideally in each Key Stage or more. And many do. These are occasions to talk about the differences between the 'original' and printed and virtual reproductions and to appreciate the scale of works of art in spaces that are designed to exhibit them in the best conditions. It is a time for pupils to encounter the 'hand' of the artist, seeing with their own eyes the qualities of the materials the artwork is made out of and how the artist has manipulated these. I also believe these visits should form part of a cultural entitlement for all children during their formal education, particularly visiting some of the publicly owned collections across Britain. Housed in our capital city at the National Gallery, the National Portrait Gallery, Tate Britain, Tate Modern, the Victoria and Albert Museum and the British Museum, and in literally thousands of regional museums and galleries, and other sites across the UK, these collections not only have some of the greatest works of art in the world in them, but they also actually belong to the children of this country, and only by seeing the objects first-hand will they gain a real sense of ownership of them. Inevitably, some children will ask, 'Can I take *my* work of art home then?', enabling you to open up discussions about the general purpose of museums and galleries, and that of publicly owned collections (see the case studies in Chapter 4), and finding out together why the pieces that you are looking at were purchased, commissioned or donated to the country.

Having your class go on an expert-led tour, or booking them into a workshop, can be a great way for them to learn about collections. In accompanying pupils on these, you can gain excellent professional development too. Be sure to communicate with the person taking the session what your objectives for the pupils are at least several weeks before the trip. The visit needs to clearly connect to the work that the children are doing at school. Tell the museum or gallery expert which curriculum subject areas you are concentrating on and your theme. Explain which work, or works, of art in their collection you have selected as stimuli, and which skills you would like pupils to develop during their time at the gallery or museum. Analysing and interpreting meaning in works of art are skills that can very effectively be improved through sessions that take place in front of original artwork. As some children can behave differently outside of the classroom because they are motivated by the change in environment, you may want to emphasize your wish to the museum or gallery expert to give all pupils the chance to speak in the non-school setting. During the tour or workshop, it will be important for you to observe the confidence pupils show in doing this and how carefully they listen to what the expert says. You should also describe to the expert how you are intending to follow up the experience back at school, with the expectation that they will impart this information to the pupils in the session.

Opting for a self-guided visit means that you can fully focus on what you want the pupils to learn, especially if you have taken advantage of any prior training offered by the museum or gallery so that you feel confident that you have a good grounding in the exhibits you want to look at. Be warned, though, that other visitors might want to see the same works of art as you, or, for reasons of conservation, loaning or photography, the work might not be on display. It would be extremely disappointing to organize a trip to see one work of art that was not on show. It is always good to have a 'Plan B'. Think about other pieces in the museum or gallery that have a comparable message, tell a similar story, use the same media and techniques, or are by the same artist. Also bear in mind that works can sometimes be placed in areas that are inaccessible to large groups. All these things should be thought through and discussed with the institution in advance.

The best way of gaining a whole group's attention when showing them an original work of art is to sit them in front of it, but do check that everyone has a good view. Some museums and galleries have portable folding stools that you can borrow or hire, but the floor will usually be suitable, unless the work of art is very tall or hung very high. Think about what height the work of art was intended to be viewed from. Have a brief list of the main points that you would like the pupils to know about the artwork and use this to steer your collective examination. First, ask lots of open-ended questions to find out what the pupils already know. Reply to any assumptions made by asking pupils to talk through their thinking. Stereotypes should also be challenged. Avoid going off at tangents, and especially tangents of tangents! Always bring the questioning back to the artwork and the list of main points that you want the children to consider. If you are extending the talk by looking at other works of art, ask pupils to make connections between them. Are the pieces made out of the same materials? Were they produced in the same period or in the same country? Is there a thematic thread?

Some museums and galleries may ask you to divide the party into small supervised groups. If this is the case, then you could provide a list of prompts to the adults taking the groups around. Ask them to look out for specific pieces of artwork and couple this information with the main points that you want the pupils to discuss about each, with links to other pieces with similar themes. To intrigue pupils into wanting to find out about the artworks for themselves, you could tell them that they are 'investigators' on an assignment and that they need to report back to base at a certain time (base being school). Just like detectives who discover evidence in a police inquiry, or how an archaeologist slowly unearths items of interest in a dig, layer by layer, so can pupils look for clues in works of art. The following questions will help children to observe, reason and compare:

- What do you think the artwork is made of?
- Why do you think it was made?
- How does it make you feel?
- Who or what do you think the artist wants the viewer to look at first?
- Can you date the artwork (with or without looking at the information label)?
- Are the marks made by the artist similar to any other marks on other pieces of art in the gallery or museum?
- What would you entitle the piece?

If at all possible, trips to see original works of art should happen at the beginning of a project to allow pupils to use their first-hand experiences to inform subsequent learning. However, if this is not practical, a trip in the middle or at the end of a project can be used to consolidate learning and act as a motivating end goal. As with any learning activity, you need to ask if and when it maximizes opportunities for pupils to develop the knowledge and skills that you have identified.

Bringing reproductions of artwork to life

First-hand experiences of original artwork are obviously important in engaging pupils in the visual arts. A painting is so much more than an accomplished set of brush marks, as is a sculpture more than a mass of carved or modelled materials. A level of awe comes from standing in front of a piece of art because the artist is communicating their ideas, passion, and endeavour directly at you. Seeing 'an original' is a feeling that is impossible to replicate in a reproduction, but there are certain things that you can do to bring a flat printed poster or digital image to life.

Role-play areas – Encourage imaginative play and interpretation by building an area in the classroom that helps children to 'step into' a picture or 'be part of' a sculpture. The Edgar Degas boat at St Mary's School in Bodmin, based on *Beach Scene* (*c*.1868–77) by Degas (see page 39), is an excellent example of how this type of immersive experience can work well. The *Katie's Picture Show* series by the author and illustrator James Mayhew employs this idea and would be a useful initial resource for inspiration. The most successful role-play areas enable children to develop a variety of skills and involve them in the designing and making of the environment. It is important not to think of role-play areas as only being suitable for the youngest children in a school. Areas that facilitate role play can stimulate pupils of all ages.

Interactive displays – Put on view in a classroom at child-height all the resources connected to the project, including printed reproductions, themed books and appropriate objects. Include a magnifying glass for studying these closely. Sometimes, artists incorporate minute messages for the very observant viewer. It can be fascinating to see what characters are getting up to in the background of a picture, or to look for hidden symbols. Very large reproductions can be purchased of some works of art (although these are expensive) big enough to cover a floor or wall and detailed enough to see the smallest of content. Enlarging content can also be achieved by having an iPad or computer as part of an interactive display, opened to the page of the museum or gallery (or archive) that the work of art is housed in. In addition to a virtual reproduction, a number of these websites have the facility to zoom in on works of art. This allows the viewer to see signs of ageing on a piece, such as cracking or peeling, and possible marks made by conservationists when restoring them. Many of these marks are not noticeable with the naked eye.

To make visible pupils' interactions with the set of stimuli, mind maps and Post-it notes, or any other way of recording pupils' thoughts, can be placed in the same area. Pupils can produce multi-sensory responses by creating 'soundscapes' (making the sounds that one might hear if we 'listen' to a work of art) or 'smellscapes' (making the smells of a work of art if one were to sniff it). Thinking about how to enable a visually impaired person to experience a work of art can be a good starting point for an activity. Massive reproductions of artwork can be made by pupils in the form of models or pictures that can be displayed in the classroom or somewhere else in the school. People could be encouraged to collect objects that relate to these, perhaps labelling each with a message from the person who brought it in saying why it is relevant. Pupils could curate these into a school museum.

Hot seating – This teaching activity allows pupils to take it in turns to be a character from a work of art, with their peers asking them questions. It helps to develop literacy skills, where pupils use their imaginations to structure stories and use vocabulary that might be applicable to a particular time and place. Hot seating develops research skills, by requiring pupils to gather, sort and select information; problem-solving skills, by getting children to hypothesize about what might be happening in a work of art, or what might happen next, by examining what is inferred by the artist; presentation skills, through pupils expressing themselves clearly; and personal development skills, by necessitating pupils to think independently and to listen to and understanding other people's ideas and perspectives. Teachers and other adults visiting the classroom can also be 'put in the hot seat' as characters from works of art for children to interview. Wearing costumes can further bring the experience to life.

Animate it – Works of art can be animated in a number of ways. A person putting on theatre make-up and a costume can be a living sculpture. By standing on a plinth, the person will instantly be turned into a work of art. I have seen this work brilliantly with the *Statue of Liberty* (1886) by Frédéric Bartholdi and *The Thinker* (1880) by Auguste Rodin. The costume could more accurately be described as a model designed to be worn. Another way to animate a work of art is to make lots of drawings of it, moving the position slightly with each subsequent drawing and making these into a cartoon. A Wacom pen tablet (as used by animator Simon Tofield, creator of *Simon's Cat*) will produce superb results, but this hardware is used by professionals and is expensive.[6] Digital software that allows you to capture pencil-on-paper drawings is a far more realistic option for the classroom, or if you have access to iPads, you could use a drawing animation app. In order to produce films of moving three-dimensional models (an example of which is discussed on pages 41–2), you will need to use stop-motion animation software. Zu3D is designed for children to use and is popular with schools,[7] but there are many other packages on the market.

Pupil sketchbooks

Pupils' involvement with any of these activities should be recorded in personal sketchbooks if possible, together with their individual mind maps. As with my recommendation for you to keep a sketchbook, to make concrete your thoughts, pupils also benefit tremendously from gathering their ideas in one place, noting the journey that they take through a project. This is evidence of their attainment, which helps them and you to assess their progress to date, aiding future learning. Ofsted reported in *Making a Mark: Art, Craft and Design 2008–11*, 'Where achievement was good or outstanding, pupils' strong understanding of how well they were doing was reinforced by regular use of sketchbooks to develop ideas, record observations, explore different media or evaluate their work' (Ofsted 2012a: 10).

Sketchbooks enable pupils to show their personal interaction with a project. They can include:

- mind maps;
- observations throughout the project in words and in sketches;
- experimentations with media;
- collections of materials, leaflets, cuttings from magazines, etc. that are relevant to the project;
- photographs of experiences during the project and reflective comments about these (for example, step-by step images of the making of a work of art (showing evaluation and modifications), recording presentations (those made to a small group, the whole class, the school, or wider community), and visits to museums and galleries); and
- evidence of directed and self-directed tasks completed at home.

To increase pupils' confidence in being able to express their ideas visually, they need to have confidence in their ability to draw. As already discussed, the basis of any artwork, be it a painting, a sculpture, a piece of textiles, or any other art form, is drawing. With the aim of improving an individual's ability to draw, here are a few simple activities for pupils to have a go at. You might want to try them out too.

Möbius curve drawings – I use this exercise to prove to people that they can draw. The principle is that the Möbius curve is a strange and unfamiliar object, and therefore it has to be continuously looked at in order to be drawn. Named after the German mathematician August Ferdinand Möbius, the curve curiously only has one side, yet is a three-dimensional object. To make one, you will need a strip of paper approximately 25 cm in length and 3 cm wide. Give the strip a half-twist and join the ends together with some sticky tape. It is now ready to draw. Leaving the curve in one position, study it and record what you see with small sketching lines in pencil (HB or 2B) on a piece of paper, or ideally straight into a sketchbook so that progress can be documented and kept. Change the position of the curve after a few minutes to make a second drawing, and then repeat again to do a third. Number the drawings and evaluate which of them has the more convincing three-dimensional qualities. To add more complexity to the exercise, make the Möbius curve from newspaper, or put tone into the drawing by shading the areas where there is little or no light.

Bug drawings – This activity can be used to aid the Möbius curve exercise if someone is struggling to make a convincing drawing that looks three-dimensional. The principle of continuously looking at what is being drawn is the same. This time, the person drawing needs to imagine that a small bug of some description (giving the bug a name appeals to young children) is crawling around the contours of an object. The job of the drawer is to track the bug's journey by drawing it on paper, like a map. Do not worry if lines are crossed over, or doubled back on, as this makes the drawing appear more three-dimensional. When finished, the drawing will resemble a wire-framed sculpture. Drawing in a biro or felt pen can work very well because it overcomes concerns about getting the lines 'wrong' and wanting to rub them out.

Talk and draw – This exercise gets pupils to describe objects in words before describing them in a drawing. For best results, at least at first, give pupils objects that they are unfamiliar with (as in the Möbius curve drawing activity). This will ensure that they have to look very closely at what they are drawing instead of using a system of visual symbols (as discussed in Chapter 2 – like drawing a flower in terms of a circle with four semicircles around the circumference for petals and a horizontal line for a stem). Pupils should be encouraged to hold the object, observe it from all angles, and to talk to a partner about the textures and shapes that they can see. Here, you could support children's learning by asking them to select the most accurate words from a bank that has been preselected and discussed with the class, or similes can be used, with descriptions such as 'it is as rough as sandpaper' or 'it is as smooth and cold as a pebble'. Only after lots of examination should pupils attempt to make a drawing of the object. Ask them to make a linear (line-only) drawing, and, when finished, they can use mark-making techniques to illustrate texture, such as dots, dashes and shading. Another good exercise is to see how many different marks can be made from one pencil and to use descriptive names for these, such as 'bumpy', 'spiky' and 'soft'. A follow-up 'talk and draw' exercise is to show an object to just a few children in the class, and for them to talk the other pupils through drawing it. The quality of the description given, and the ability of the drawers to listen to instructions, will determine how well the drawings mimic the original object.

Shared drawings – Making the first mark on a sheet of white paper can be rather intimidating, especially in a brand new pristine sketchbook. A worthwhile exercise to overcome this preciousness is to draw on a drawing that has already been started by someone else. This collaboration can happen on several taped-together sheets of A1 sugar paper, or it could take place on a very long roll of paper (such as lining paper used for decorating homes) that stretches the length of the school hall, where everyone is invited to make a contribution. It is a good idea to suggest a theme so that the final piece tells some sort of story. For example, 'My journey to school' would work well. You could also look at works of art that have been produced on a long length, such as the eleventh-century *Bayeux Tapestry* or Chinese hand scrolls, such as *Spring Morning in the Han Palace* (*c*.1540) by Qiu Ying. Both of these have narratives that the viewer can 'read' almost like a soap opera.

Another idea could be to have six or seven separate very large pieces of paper on the floor of a classroom or school hall, each with an interesting object in the middle, perhaps linked to a particular project theme. Pupils can then be asked to make first-hand observational drawings of the objects, one at a time, before moving on to the next sheet of paper.

Notes

1   Culture 24 is an online service funded by Arts Council England and the Department for Education listing cultural events in many museums, galleries, heritage sites and archives in the UK and can be accessed online at: www.culture24.org.uk/home.
2   The Space is a digital arts media service from the Arts Council England in partnership with the BBC and can be accessed online at: http://thespace.org/.
3   Bridgeman Art Library is available at: www.bridgemanart.com.
4   The Your Paintings online database is available at: www.bbc.co.uk/arts/yourpaintings.
5   Google Art Project is available at: www.googleartproject.com/.
6   Examples of Simon Tofield's animations with a Wacom pen tablet can be seen online at: www.simonscat.com/.
7   Information about Zu3D software is available at: www.zu3d.com/.

Chapter 8

Celebrating pupils' work and sharing pedagogy

Within a progressive learning environment, pupils' achievements are recognized with soft and hard rewards being given by teachers, and other teaching support staff, to pupils for their attitude towards their learning and for the work that they produce. Visual displays, of various descriptions, can play an important role in this, and are a valuable way of documenting different stages in a project. They can be mounted in a classroom, acting as a form of communication between teachers and their pupils, shared with a whole school, or exhibited to a wider audience beyond the school walls. If the work chosen to display is selected through a process of ongoing evaluation with pupils, showing where achievement in a class has been most evident, this can have multiple educational benefits:

- It can boost an individual's confidence and self-esteem, encouraging pupils to work hard and strive for higher goals.
- It enables other pupils to see what achievement looks like, valuing the progress that pupils make, as well as their attainment.
- It documents progression made by individuals, by a class and by a school, and creates a visual history that can be archived.
- It communicates with visitors and the wider public what happens in a school.
- It helps to develop pedagogical approaches by professionals learning from each other's practice.

The nature of a display depends on the type of expected learning outcomes, and the objectives and the design of the project. Consider in your planning how different ways of celebrating pupils' work helps them to demonstrate their understanding of what they have learnt, and how these ways relate to the original learning objectives. For example, if you were to choose mounting an exhibition at your school as a way of celebrating pupils' final outcomes from a cross-curricular project, how might organizing the exhibition develop pupils' literacy, numeracy, problem-solving, evaluation, presentation and personal development skills? Will pupils be involved in deciding where the exhibition is staged in the school and in thinking about how it might be physically laid out and curated? Could they take a lead in inviting guests? Are there opportunities for different groups of children to work in teams and to take responsibility for certain tasks? Or might a different type of display, such as a looped presentation on a digital screen in a communal area of the school, be a more appropriate way to show other people pupils' achievements? Perhaps posting outcomes on the school website would work well, with pupils writing blogs or creating podcasts, or would producing a publication be more effective?

Celebrating process as well as final outcomes

Documenting the process that children go through to produce their final outcomes is vitally important for assessment. This is where you will be able to see how much progress individual pupils have made from the beginning of a task to its completion. As well as pupils using sketchbooks to record this (as described in Chapter 7), a display area in a classroom that can capture the development of the project from a whole-class perspective can be extremely helpful. Alongside resources connected to the project (physical and virtual reproductions, objects, books), an interactive display (see pages 92–3), incorporating a collaborative mind map expressing pupils' thoughts and ideas (see page 88), can also include an area for pupils' 'work in progress'. This can be a space where, at the end of a lesson, the teacher or pupils can post one or several pieces of work that show particular promise, perhaps a piece voted for by the children, or one that has been shared with the class on a visualizer. Another area on the interactive classroom display could celebrate work that pupils have produced independently from school, at home or in an after-school club, that is linked to the theme of the project. By clearly labelling the sections of the display, everyone will know how each part connects to another; which is finished pupils' work, which is 'work in progress', and which things are resources. This whole display can act as a central communication point between staff and pupils. It will map a project's journey, pinpointing milestones where the project presently is, and where it might lead. Parents also may appreciate being kept informed about the project via this display too.

Positioned in communal areas of a school, printed books and digital screens that present photographically how a project is progressing, together with the final outcomes of a project when it is finished, can mark the achievements of individuals and a class to the whole school. Advertising the school in this way to perspective parents and other visitors means that they can see what happens during lesson times when waiting in reception. The books and displays also make excellent memory aids for the pupils. They will enjoy talking through their experiences of a project using the photographs to their own parents or carers, or pupils from different classes at break times, and will feel a great sense of satisfaction, boosting their confidence, and whetting their appetite to do more of the same.

These books and digital displays (as well as class website pages) can be put together by pupils, helping to develop their literacy and presentation skills using technology. One successful strategy is to have a rolling programme during the year where a different team of pupils take responsibility to digitally document a project photographically from beginning to end, gathering comments from people involved throughout. On the school website, the photographs and comments can form part of a regular blog, providing a motivating purpose for writing. The page can be a great way to share digital animations too, if these happen to be final outcomes.

Looking at a physical book is a very different experience from seeing something on a screen, having the advantage of being able to be held in the hand and passed around from person to person. These can be produced by pupils using photo albums or scrapbooks with printed labels, or they can be designed and professionally printed online by following step-by-step instructions on one of the many supermarket websites, and those of other companies, now offering affordable photo book services.

Physical exhibitions

Physical exhibitions can be an impressive way to present children's work. An in-school exhibition can be put up in a communal area, such as a library or foyer, or the school hall can be taken over. The outside space in a school could be used too. The opening can be performed with some ceremony as part of a special assembly, or an evening private view could be arranged, inviting guests from the local community, along with the pupils' families. Some schools use these events as fundraisers, selling framed artwork, raffle tickets and alike. Companies specialize in framing services for schools, some on a no sale, no fee basis.

It can be possible to mount exhibitions that reach out to a greater number of local people by asking permission to use empty shop window space, or a town hall. Events of this type can generate very welcome positive feedback that improves community cohesion.

You may want to link your exhibition to a regional or national initiative. A popular annual scheme is called the Big Draw,[1] organized by the Campaign for Learning, with awards given to the most creative drawing events happening in schools across the country. If you are teaching pupils over the age of 7, it is well worth looking at the prospect of becoming an Arts Award[2] centre. Run by Trinity College London, and overseen by Arts Council England, the Arts Award programme facilitates young people in developing their creativity through five certificated criteria-led levels. There is also a separate option to apply for Artsmark status, which is a national recognition of the quality of arts provision in your school.

Participating in such initiatives is fantastically motivating for schools. Submitting work to an external body makes people want to produce something of real quality. If pieces of work are selected to be shown as examples of good practice with other schools, it can provide a genuine lift to morale in a school. If that good practice is exhibited in a collective, prestigious event the excitement can give everyone involved an immense feeling of pride. When I have been with teachers and parents on these occasions at Take One Picture or Picture This! private views, they have been noticeably moved by seeing their children's work being so highly valued, many to tears.

Online opportunities that can lead to improving pedagogy

At the beginning of this book, I talked about the seemingly endless possibilities that an encounter with a work of art can lead to. When seeing a piece that interests us, it might prompt lively discussion, further enquiry, and perhaps result in producing personal responses, maybe in the form of another visual artwork, or a piece of music, dance, drama or writing. The Internet not only assists with these encounters by enabling people to access a wide range of artistic cultural works online (we now have unprecedented virtual entry into collections all over the world), but it also offers a platform where we can view other people's creative responses to artworks and share our own.

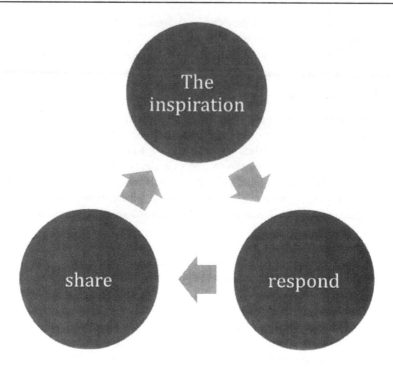

Figure 8.1 The cycle of creativity.

Some museum, gallery and archive websites interact with their users by crowdsourcing information about their collections. Personal insights can reveal fascinating perspectives. Using such websites with pupils helps them to understand that knowledge is socially constructed and that alternative viewpoints are valid. Websites that encourage people to submit their creative ideas and work linked to cultural collections help in demonstrating that everyone can play their part in a cycle of creativity that connects people across time, place and cultures. The Take One Picture website (see page 35) is an example where this works well, and, for teachers, this resource makes them aware of different pedagogical approaches that have been successful in real-life educational settings.

Figure 8.1 illustrates how the cycle of creativity happens. An original inspiration (such as a highly accomplished masterpiece or an ancient artefact) can inspire a personal response. When this is shared with others online, it has the potential of being viewed by many thousands of people from across the world. This response can then become an inspiration itself for others to respond to. And so the cycle continues.

The Internet has revolutionized how someone might find an *inspiration* and how he or she can *share* his or her creative responses. However, the same artistic process has taken place since people first started using charcoal to make pictures on the walls of caves representing animals. On seeing one of these, someone at the time, no doubt, would have used the idea to produce his or her own version of it; not identical, but a transcription of it styled by his or her own personality. People have always been influenced by the artwork of others. Most works of art are never entirely truly original because, either consciously or unconsciously, they are likely to be based on art that someone has seen before. Even if an artwork is a reaction against another work of art, or group of artworks, that the artist dislikes, it is a subversion of it, and therefore is still within the cycle of creativity.

Accounts of famous artists paying homage to other artists' work are common. Contemporary artists refer back to past masters, and past masters delve into the history of art for their inspiration. We know that Constable adored the paintings of Rubens, in particular his landscapes, and that Rubens was heavily influenced by artists from the early Renaissance, such as Piero della Francesca. We know that Turner was fixated by the sunsets of Claude Lorrain, and that Joseph Wright of Derby's chiaroscuro technique (strong contrasts between light and dark) came from seeing the work of Caravaggio.

Modern-day artists, such as Tom Hunter and Sam Taylor-Wood, Laura Ford and Richard Billingham, bring new perspectives to familiar works of art produced many years ago by creating updated versions of them, using photography, video, sculpture and painting. Poets such as U.A. Fanthorpe (see Chapter 3) have been inspired by works of art enough to produce their own pieces in another form. And novelists too, such as Tracy Chevalier and Sally Vickers, have taken specific works of art to imaginatively weave plots around, with film directors transcribing these for the cinema.

On the Internet, you will be able to trace many more examples of where artists have been influenced by other artists' work. Whereas Constable and Turner needed to seek out the original paintings of Rubens and Claude Lorrain in galleries, you can do your research in the comfort of your own home or classroom. And better still, you can share your own and your pupils' responses to these works, and others, via the Internet to audiences across the globe.

To maximize the pedagogical benefits of sharing learning outcomes stimulated by a work of art, if at all possible, it is a good idea to make contact with the museum, gallery or archive where the work is held, with the aim of showing the work on their website or making a link from their website to your school's. If they do not already run a scheme that encourages such educational interaction with their collections, it might be the case that your proactivity instigates a partnership for your school or sets in motion the beginnings of a programme that could inspire many more teachers to use the visual arts across the curriculum.

Notes

1   Information about the Big Draw annual events and resources can be found at: www.campaignfordrawing.org/bigdraw/.
2   More information about the Arts Award and Artsmark programmes can be found at: www.artsaward.org.uk/ and www.artsmark.org.uk/.

Chapter 9

Conclusion

The principal message that I have sought to convey in this book is that art appreciation and the making of art should be taught as one and the same. We have much to learn from the work of artists, and by being involved in learning about and by creating art ourselves we can all partake in a process that connects people across time, place and cultures.

Examples throughout the book clearly show that it is not necessary for a teacher to be an expert in either art-making or Art History in order to use the visual arts across the curriculum. Small amounts of information about artistic techniques or works of art can capture the imaginations of pupils, staff and members of a school's wider community, and, if time is allowed for ideas to develop, exciting and educationally meaningful projects can emerge.

That there is so much room for interpretation with the visual arts makes using them such a rich resource for learning about the world in which we live and for finding out about ourselves. This quality should also make teachers and pupils secure in the knowledge that there is no one right or wrong way of looking at art, and indeed by considering different viewpoints we open our minds to endless creative possibilities.

An Initial Teacher Training student from Northampton University, where I lecture, summed up these points perfectly when she reflected on a series of art sessions that she had taken as part of her degree:

> I had not studied Art for well over two decades before this module at university. My perception of myself as an artist was quite lacking. Through the sessions, however, I realized that actually art is not about how technically good someone's skills are; rather, it is about being creative, using things (artists' work, real-life objects, etc.) to motivate and inspire and to make a personal interpretation. My responsibility as a teacher is to make children aware of that.

During this module, the teacher training students learnt how to develop a cross-curricular project focused around the visual arts. They were encouraged to think about the specific needs that children in a class may have and how the activities that they design might help each pupil to make progress. They discussed how planning needs to take into account strategies for assessing and using pupils' prior knowledge, how to most effectively engage children by making their learning relevant to their experiences and interests, and how to help children to become autonomous learners and team players, encouraging curiosity and promoting a love of learning. Furthermore, the students looked at how their plans fulfilled and enhanced the requirements of the National Curriculum across a variety of subject areas.

By designing short- and medium-term cross-curricular plans, the trainee teachers were more able to accurately critique what outstanding teaching looks like, making them more equipped to advance an educational culture that thrives on individuality, creativity and a passion of learning.

Research published in *How the World's Most Improved School Systems Keep Getting Better* (Mourshed *et al.* 2010) by the global management consulting firm McKinsey and Company, a follow-up to *How the World's Best-performing Schools Come out on Top* (Barber and Mourshed 2007), also published by McKinsey & Company, shows that there is good reason to encourage teachers and teacher training students to shape instructional practice themselves. School systems in the world that enable teachers to do this are on an 'improvement journey' from 'good to great' and 'great to excellent'. At the report launch conference (streamed online), debates centred on the importance of ensuring a positive professional culture in schools, where the climate is one of sharing common goals, enjoying collective responsibility (as opposed to top-down accountability) and embedding collaboration in everyday working practice among staff and pupils. As we have seen, the Take One Picture and Picture This! models very effectively facilitate a culture of collaboration between teachers, children and others with an interest in education (for example, parents, university lecturers, and museum and gallery education staff). These two schemes help to install a level of passion in teaching and improve pupil outcomes.

There is considerable evidence in the case studies in Part II, and in the various reports that I have highlighted in Part I, that the visual arts can positively affect pupil performance across many subject areas. However, it is apparent, particularly in times of financial austerity, when the place of the arts is repeatedly questioned, and when funding for the arts is at its lowest, that more needs to be done in persuading policymakers about the contribution that the visual arts can play in engaging learners through common themes and skills and why the visual arts are a fundamental component of any education. The Cambridge Primary Review states, 'Authoritative official enquiries on the arts, creativity and culture are warmly applauded and then disappear without trace [but] Those primary schools which do not allow vulnerable subjects to be marginalized are those which are confident and knowledgeable about their value and which have expertise to teach them well' (Alexander 2010: 252).

Publications such as Ofsted's (2011) *Good Practice Resource – The Journey to Excellence in Art, Craft and Design: Battyeford C of E Primary School* report in detail how schools go about making significant changes to the design of their curriculum and the learning culture in their schools. When newly appointed, Diane Pyatt, Head Teacher of Battyeford Primary School, Kirklees, West Yorkshire, decided that even though standards in the school were above average, to make them outstanding she had to make some significant changes. She and her staff wanted to give pupils more opportunities to develop their creative skills and, in so doing, increasing their independence as learners and confidence in their own abilities. Everyone shared the vision that the visual arts were the key to achieving these aims:

> Before we placed art, craft and design at the heart of what we do, pupils' achievements were above average, but there was not enough 'wow' or 'awe and

wonder' in what they did. Compliant and hard-working pupils have transformed into creative, enthusiastic, self-confident, discerning and highly able pupils; not only in art, craft and design but also in other subjects. Their communication and cooperative skills are exceptional because of the way they are encouraged to work together, talk about their work and make decisions based on their developing understanding of materials, forms and genre across all dimensions of the subject. Our school is a vibrant community, not least due to high-quality teaching and the excellent partnerships with artists, craftworkers, designers, local galleries and parents.

Three things were put in place to enable this to happen:

- Half-termly themes were enhanced by linking them to the work of artists, including internationally renowned contemporary artists, artists from the past and local creative practitioners.
- Making use of local galleries and other art venues.
- Flexible timetabling, including special days and weeks dedicated to the themes and the visual arts.

We need to hear more from teachers about real-life practice in schools where the impact of the visual arts has been most marked. Sharing professional practice through publications (printed and online), at conferences and in exhibitions about exactly how the visual arts are used to improve educational performance gives other teachers ideas for driving improvement in their schools. The development of pedagogy needs to belong to teachers. The cultural sector can help by giving more prominence to educational interactions with the visual arts on gallery and museum and other arts organization websites, and in physical exhibition spaces too.

Notwithstanding all of the interlinking reasons why the visual arts should be at the heart of a school's curriculum, it is still the fact that what compels me to work with teachers and teacher training students, enthusing about art, is that I simply love art, and I hope that they will want to impart their own enthusiasm about it to their pupils. I love all kinds of art. New and old. Made by artists from different places around the world and from just around the corner from where I live. I genuinely do not understand people who do not get excited by art, but then, I suppose that is the definition of a passion, is it not? Art ignites powerful emotions in me, it conveys things that I cannot put into words and it compels me to find out more. It makes me who I am.

References

Alexander, R. (ed.) (2010) *Children, Their World, Their Education: Final Report and Recommendations of the Cambridge Review*, London: Routledge.

Barber, M. and Mourshed, M. (2007) *How the World's Best-performing Schools Come Out on Top*, New York: McKinsey & Company, available at: http://mckinseyonsociety.com/topics/education/ (accessed 10 October 2012).

Bruner, J. (1960) *The Process of Education*, Cambridge, MA: Harvard University Press (revised edition 1977).

Callaghan, J. (1976) 'Towards a national debate', text of speech delivered 18 October 1976, reprinted in *The Guardian*, 15 October 2001, available at: http://education.guardian.co.uk/thegreatdebate/story/0,9860,574645,00.html (accessed 4 October 2013).

Calouste Gulbenkian Foundation (1982) *The Arts in Schools*, London: BPCC Oyez Press.

Deasy, R.J. (2005) *Third Space: When Learning Matters*, Washington, DC: Arts Education Partnership.

Department for Culture, Media and Sport & Department for Education (2012) *Cultural Education in England: An Independent Review by Darren Henley for the Department for Culture, Media and Sport & Department for Education*, London: HMSO.

Department for Education (2012a) *Statutory Framework for the Early Years Foundation Stage*, London: HMSO, available at: http://media.education.gov.uk/assets/files/pdf/e/eyfs%20statutory%20framework%20march%202012.pdf (accessed 11 December 2012).

Department for Education (2012b) *Teachers' Standards*, London: HMSO, available at: www.education.gov.uk/publications/eOrderingDownload/teachers%20standards.pdf (accessed 12 October 2012).

Dewey, J. (1938) *Experience and Education*, New York: Touchstone (first Touchstone edition published 1997).

DfEE (1998) *The National Literacy Strategy: Framework for Teaching*, London: DfEE.

DfEE (1999) *The National Numeracy Strategy: Framework for Teaching Mathematics from Reception to Year 6*, London: DfEE.

Downing, D., Johnson, F. and Kaur, S. (2003) *Saving a Place for the Arts? A Survey of the Arts in Primary Schools in England*, Berkshire, UK: The National Foundation for Educational Research (NfER).

Fanthorpe, U.A. (2010) *New and Collected Poems*, London: Enitharmon Press.

Gardner, H. (1993) *Multiple Intelligences: The Theory in Practice*, New York: Basic Books.

Howard-Jones, P.A. *et al.* (2005) 'Semantic divergence and creative story generation: an fMRI investigation', *Cognitive Brain Research*, 25: 240–50, available at: www.sciencedirect.com/science/article/pii/S0926641005001631 (accessed 15 September 2013).

Lowenfeld, V. (1947) *Creative and Mental Growth*, New York: Macmillan.

Luquet, G.H. (1913) *Les Dessins d'un Enfant*, Paris: Alcan.

Malaguzzi, L. (1998) 'No Way. The Hundred is There', in C. Edwards, L. Gandini and G. Forman (eds), *The Hundred Languages of Children: The Reggio Emilia Approach – Advanced Reflections* (2nd edition), London: Ablex Publishing.

Mourshed, M., Chijioke, C. and Barber, M. (2010) *How the World's Most Improved School Systems Keep Getting Better*, New York: McKinsey & Company, available at: http://mckinseyon society.com/topics/education/ (accessed 8 November 2012).

NACCCE (1999) *All Our Futures: Creativity, Culture and Education*, London: HMSO, available at: http://sirkenrobinson.com/pdf/allourfutures.pdf (accessed 10 September 2013).

Ofsted (2010) *Learning: Creative Approaches that Raise Standards*, London: HMSO, available at: www.ofsted.gov.uk/resources/learning-creative-approaches-raise-standards (accessed 9 September 2012).

Ofsted (2011) *Good Practice Resource – The Journey to Excellence in Art, Craft and Design: Battyeford C of E Primary School*, London: HMSO, available at: www.ofsted.gov.uk/ resources/good-practice-resource-journey-excellence-art-craft-and-design-battyeford-cofe-primary-school (accessed 5 August 2012).

Ofsted (2012a) *Making a Mark: Art, Craft and Design 2008–11*, London: HMSO, available at: www.ofsted.gov.uk/resources/making-mark-art-craft-and-design-education-2008-11 (accessed 1 July 2012).

Ofsted (2012b) *Schools Inspection Handbook*, London: HMSO, available at: www.ofsted.gov.uk/ resources/school-inspection-handbook-september-2012 (accessed 10 November 2012).

Piaget, J.P. (1952) *The Origins of Intelligence in Children*, New York: International Universities Press.

Plowden, B. *et al.* (1967) *Children and Their Primary Schools: A Report of the Central Advisory Council for Education (England)*, London: HMSO.

RCMG (2007) *Inspiration, Identity, Learning: The Value of Museums, Second Study*, Leicester, UK: University of Leicester.

Read, H. (1958) *Education Through Art*, London: Faber Research Centre for Museums and Galleries.

Robinson, K. (2006) *Schools Kill Creativity*, TED conference talk, available at: www.ted. com/talks/ken_robinson_says_schools_kill_creativity.html (accessed 16 September 2013).

Robinson, K. (2011) *Out of Our Minds* (2nd revised edition), Chichester, UK: Capstone.

Rose, J. (2009) *The Independent Review of the Primary Curriculum: Final Report*, London: DCSF, available at: www.education.gov.uk/publications/eOrderingDownload/Primary_curriculum_ Report.pdf (accessed 9 August 2012).

Rowland, C. (director and producer) (2010) *We Are the People We've Been Waiting For*, available at: www.wearethepeoplemovie.com (accessed 11 May 2012).

Slater, A. (2006) *Take One Picture Evaluation Report*, Greenwich, University of Greenwich Business School.

Storrie, J. (1990) *Elephants in Royal Leamington Spa*. Leamington Spa, UK: Weird Books.

Thornton, L. and Brunton, P. (2009) *Understanding the Reggio Approach: Early Years Education in Practice*, London: Routledge.

Training and Development Agency for Schools (2002) *Qualifying to Teach: Professional Standards for Qualified Teacher Status and Requirements for Initial Teacher Training*, London: TDA.

The Trustees of the National Gallery (2007) *The National Gallery Review: April 2006–March 2007*, London: National Gallery Company. www.nationalgallery.org.uk/upload/pdf/NG_ Review_06-07.pdf (accessed 30 October 2013).Vygotsky, L.S. (1978) *Mind in Society: The Development of Higher Psychological Processes*, Cambridge, MA: Harvard University Press.

Wyse, D. and McGarty, L. (2009) *The National Gallery Initial Teacher Education Cultural Placement Partnership: A Research Evaluation*, Cambridge, UK: University of Cambridge Faculty of Education.

Wyse, D. and McGarty, L. (2010) *The National Gallery Picture in Focus Project: A Research Evaluation*, Cambridge, UK: University of Cambridge Faculty of Education.

Referenced works of art and where to find them

I have purposefully used examples of artwork in this book that are easily accessible online. It is always best to use a digital reproduction produced by the collection that holds the artwork, or a database that has been given permission by the holding collection to distribute the reproduction, to ensure the copyright laws have been adhered to and that the quality of the reproduction is as near to the original as possible. Poor-quality reproductions, which lack detail and clarity (due to having a resolution that is too low), and where the dimensions or colours are distorted, can be difficult to teach with and can disengage pupils. If an artwork is being used for a sustained piece of work, a physical print of the reproduction should be used alongside any digital image to aid recall when the whiteboard or individual computers are switched off.

An Allegory of the Vanities of Human Life, c.1640, Harmen Steenwyck, National Gallery, London, available at: www.nationalgallery.org.uk/paintings/harmen-steenwyck-still-life-an-allegory-of-the-vanities-of-human-life (accessed 10 September 2013).

An Experiment on a Bird in the Air Pump, 1768, Joseph Wright of Derby, National Gallery, London, available at: www.nationalgallery.org.uk/paintings/joseph-wright-of-derby-an-experiment-on-a-bird-in-the-air-pump (accessed 10 September 2013).

Asleep on the Watch, 1872, John Thomas Peele, Rotherham Museums and Art Galleries, available at: www.bbc.co.uk/arts/yourpaintings/paintings/asleep-on-the-watch-69336 (accessed 10 September 2013).

Beach Scene, c.1868–77, Edgar Degas, National Gallery, London, available at: www.nationalgallery.org.uk/paintings/hilaire-germain-edgar-degas-beach-scene (accessed 10 September 2013).

Combing the Hair, 1896, Edgar Degas, National Gallery, London, available at: www.nationalgallery.org.uk/paintings/hilaire-germain-edgar-degas-combing-the-hair-la-coiffure (accessed 10 September 2013).

David, 1500–4, Michelangelo, Galleria dell'Accademia, Florence, available at: www.polomuseale.firenze.it/en/musei/?m=accademia (accessed 10 September 2013).

Equivalent VIII, 1966, Carl Andre, Tate, London, available at: www.tate.org.uk/art/artworks/andre-equivalent-viii-t01534 (accessed 10 September 2013).

Exhibition of a Rhinoceros at Venice, c.1751, Pietro Longhi, National Gallery, London, available at: www.nationalgallery.org.uk/paintings/pietro-longhi-exhibition-of-a-rhinoceros-at-venice (accessed 10 September 2013).

Fountain, 1917, Marcel Duchamp, original lost, replica made 1964, Tate, London, available at: www.tate.org.uk/art/artworks/duchamp-fountain-t07573 (accessed 10 September 2013).

Guernica, 1937, Pablo Picasso, Museo Nacional Centro de Arte Reina Sofía, Madrid, available at: www.museoreinasofia.es/en/collection/artwork/guernica (accessed 10 September 2013).

Hay Wain, 1821, John Constable, National Gallery, London, available at: www.nationalgallery. org.uk/paintings/john-constable-the-hay-wain (accessed 10 September 2013).

La Trahison de Images (Ceci n'est pas une pipe), 1928–9, René Magritte, Los Angeles County Museum of Art, California, available at: http://collections.lacma.org/node/239578 (accessed 10 September 2013).

Little Dancer Aged Fourteen, 1880–1, cast *c*.1922, Edgar Degas, Tate, London, available at: www.tate.org.uk/art/artworks/degas-little-dancer-aged-fourteen-n06076 (accessed 10 September 2013).

Mona Lisa, *c*.1503–6, Leonardo da Vinci, Louvre, Paris, available at: www.louvre.fr/en/oeuvre-notices/mona-lisa-%E2%80%93-portrait-lisa-gherardini-wife-francesco-del-giocondo (accessed 10 September 2013).

Nottingham from the East, 1695, Jan Siberechts, Nottingham City Museums and Galleries, available at: www.bbc.co.uk/arts/yourpaintings/paintings/view-of-nottingham-from-the-east-46880 (accessed 10 September 2013).

Rain, Steam and Speed – The Great Western Railway, 1844, Joseph Mallord William Turner, National Gallery, London, available at: www.nationalgallery.org.uk/paintings/joseph-mallord-william-turner-rain-steam-and-speed-the-great-western-railway (accessed 10 September 2013).

Robin Hood and his Merry Men Entertaining Richard the Lionheart in Sherwood Forest, 1839, Daniel Maclise, Nottingham City Museums and Galleries, available at: www.bbc.co.uk/arts/yourpaintings/paintings/robin-hood-and-his-merry-men-entertaining-richard-the-lion46882 (accessed 10 September 2013).

Saint George and the Dragon, *c*.1470, Paolo Uccello, National Gallery, London, available at: www.nationalgallery.org.uk/paintings/paolo-uccello-saint-george-and-the-dragon (accessed 10 September 2013).

Spiral Jetty, 1970, Robert Smithson, Great Salt Lake, Utah, available at: www.robertsmithson.com/earthworks/spiral_jetty.htm (accessed 10 September 2013).

Spring Morning in the Han Palace, *c*.1540, Qiu Ying, National Palace Museum, Taipei, Taiwan, available at: www.npm.gov.tw/en/Article.aspx?sNo=04000980 (accessed 10 September 2013).

Statue of Liberty, 1886, Frédéric Bartholdi, New York, available at: http://whc.unesco.org/en/list/307 (accessed 10 September 2013).

Sunflowers, 1888, Vincent van Gogh, National Gallery, London, available at: www.national gallery.org.uk/paintings/vincent-van-gogh-sunflowers (accessed 10 September 2013.

The Ambassadors, 1533, Hans Holbein the Younger, National Gallery, London, available at: www.nationalgallery.org.uk/paintings/hans-holbein-the-younger-the-ambassadors (accessed 10 September 2013).

The Angel of the North, 1998, Antony Gormley, Gateshead, UK, available at: www.gateshead. gov.uk/Leisure%20and%20Culture/attractions/Angel/Home.aspx (accessed 10 September 2013).

The Battle of San Romano, *c*.1438–40, Paolo Uccello, National Gallery, London, available at: www.nationalgallery.org.uk/paintings/paolo-uccello-the-battle-of-san-romano (accessed 10 September 2013).

The Castle of Muiden in Winter, 1658, Jan Beerstraaten, National Gallery, London, available at: www.nationalgallery.org.uk/paintings/jan-beerstraaten-the-castle-of-muiden-in-winter (accessed 10 September 2013).

The Goose Fair, Nottingham, 1926, Arthur Spooner, Nottingham City Museums and Galleries, available at: www.bbc.co.uk/arts/yourpaintings/paintings/the-goose-fair-nottingham-46818 (accessed 10 September 2013).

The Great Wave of Kanagawa, 1831, Katsushika Hokusai, British Museum, London, available at: www.britishmuseum.org/research/collection_online/collection_object_details.aspx?object Id=3097579&partId=1&searchText=Hokusai+Great+Wave&page=1 (accessed 10 September 2013).

The Last Supper, 1495–8, Leonardo da Vinci, Convent of Santa Maria delle Grazie, Milan, available at: http://whc.unesco.org/en/list/93 and http://whc.unesco.org/en/list/93/video (accessed 10 September 2013).

The Leam near Willes Road Bridge, Warwickshire, c.1880, Frederick Whitehead, Leamington Spa Art Gallery and Museum, available at: www.bbc.co.uk/arts/yourpaintings/paintings/the-leam-near-the-willes-road-bridge-warwickshire-54477 (accessed 10 September 2013).

The Oxley Children, c.1825, unknown artist, Rotherham Museums and Art Galleries, available at: www.bbc.co.uk/arts/yourpaintings/paintings/the-oxley-children-69437 (accessed 10 September 2013).

The Scream, 1895, Edvard Munch, National Gallery, Oslo, Norway, available at: www.nasjonal museet.no/en/collections_and_research/edvard_munch_in_the_national_museum/the_ scream/ (accessed 10 September 2013).

The Thinker, 1880, cast 1903, Auguste Rodin, Musée Rodin, Paris, available at: www.musee-rodin.fr/en/collections/sculptures/thinker (accessed 10 September 2013).

Two Boys and a Girl making Music, 1629, Jan Molenaer, National Gallery, London, available at: www.nationalgallery.org.uk/paintings/jan-miense-molenaer-two-boys-and-a-girl-making-music (accessed 10 September 2013).

Verity, 2012, Damien Hirst, Ilfracombe, north Devon, available at: www.visitilfracombe.co.uk/ homepage/verity (accessed 10 September 2013).

Wilton Diptych, c.1395–9, unknown artist, National Gallery, London, available at: www. nationalgallery.org.uk/paintings/english-or-french-the-wilton-diptych (accessed 10 September 2013).

Museums, galleries and archives

Arts Awards (online arts news), available at: www.artsaward.org.uk/ (accessed 16 September 2013).

Bridgeman (online archive), available at: www.bridgemanart.com/ (accessed 16 September 2013).

Campaign for Drawing (online arts news), available at: www.campaignfordrawing.org/bigdraw/ (accessed 16 September 2013).

Culture 24 (online arts news), available at: www.culture24.org.uk/home (accessed 16 September 2013).

Galleria dell'Accademia, Florence, available at: www.polomuseale.firenze.it/en/musei/?m=accademia (accessed 16 September 2013).

Google Art Project (online archive), available at: www.google.com/culturalinstitute/project/art-project (accessed 16 September 2013).

Leamington Spa Art Gallery and Museum, available at: www.warwickdc.gov.uk/WDC/Royal PumpRooms/Art+Gallery+and+Museum/ (accessed 16 September 2013).

Los Angeles County Museum of Art, California, available at: www.lacma.org/ (accessed 16 September 2013).

Louvre, Paris, available at: www.louvre.fr/ (accessed 16 September 2013).

Musée Rodin, Paris, available at: www.musee-rodin.fr/ (accessed 16 September 2013).

Museo Nacional Centro de Arte Reina Sofia, Madrid, available at: www.museoreinasofia.es/ (accessed 16 September 2013).

National Gallery, Oslo, available at: www.nasjonalmuseet.no/ (accessed 16 September 2013).

National Palace Museum, Taipei, Taiwan, available at: www.npm.gov.tw/ (accessed 16 September 2013).

Nottingham City Museums and Galleries, available at: www.nottinghamcity.gov.uk/article/22174/Museums-Galleries-and-Attractions (accessed 16 September 2013).

Rotherham Museums and Art Galleries, available at: www.rotherham.gov.uk/museums (accessed 16 September 2013).

Tate, London, Liverpool and St Ives, available at: www.tate.org.uk/ (accessed 16 September 2013).

The British Museum, available at: www.britishmuseum.org/ (accessed 16 September 2013).

The National Gallery, London, available at: www.nationalgallery.org.uk/ (accessed 16 September 2013).

The Space (online arts news), available at: http://thespace.org/(accessed 16 September 2013).

Your Paintings (online archive), available at: www.bbc.co.uk/arts/yourpaintings/ (accessed 16 September 2013).

Index

Note: page numbers in italic type refer to figures; those in bold type refer to tables.